초등에서
KB262847
브릿지
BRIDGE VOCA
보카
중등으로
| Intermediate |

How to Use 브릿지 보카

① 단어 학습과 Daily Test

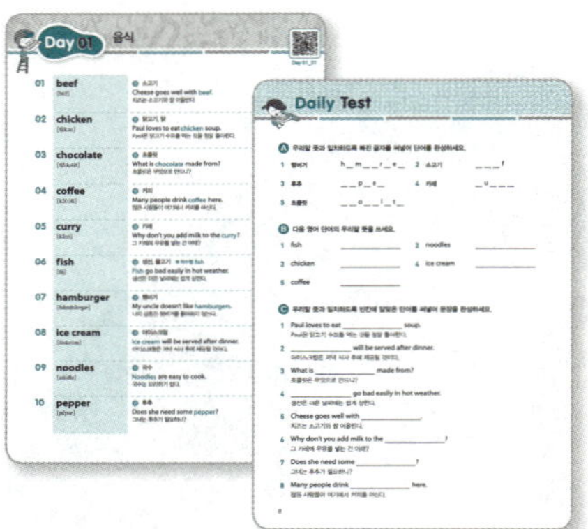

하나의 Day는 20단어로 구성되어 있습니다.
암기 부담을 줄이기 위해 10단어씩 나누어 학습합니다.
원어민의 발음으로 녹음된 단어와 예문을
QR코드를 통해 들으면서 정확한 발음을 익히고,
문장 활용 능력을 키울 수 있습니다.

② Review

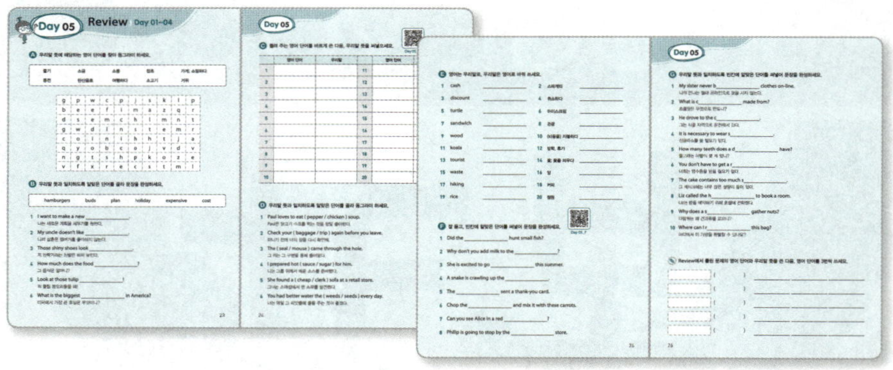

4일 학습 후 5일째에는 지금까지 배운 단어들을 확실하게 복습합니다. Word Search, 문장 완성하기,
받아쓰기 등 다양한 유형의 문제를 풀면서 단어들을 다시 한 번 머릿속에 새깁니다.

③ Index

단어들을 알파벳 순으로 수록하여,
특정 단어를 빠르게 찾을 수 있습니다.

 이 교재의 모든 음원은 메가북스 홈페이지에서
무료 MP3파일로도 다운받을 수 있습니다.

Contents와 학습 진도표

브릿지 보카 시리즈 구성

Day	권 구성	Basic	Intermediate	Advanced
01		사람	음식	활동
02		수업	동물과 식물	사물 묘사
03		취미와 여가	여행과 휴가	문화
04		음식	쇼핑	정치
05		Review	Review	Review
06		가족	장소	자연환경
07		과일과 채소	대인 관계	상황 묘사
08		동물	학교	우주와 과학
09		일상생활	나라와 지역	경제
10		Review	Review	Review
11		식물과 곤충	순서	일의 진행
12		날씨	건물과 건축물	국제 사회
13		음악	가정	상태
14		집	사회생활	생각과 인지
15	주제	Review	Review	Review
16		패션	시장	인물 묘사
17		운동	건강과 질병	위치와 방향
18		얼굴과 인물 묘사	의사소통	달력
19		감정	때와 시기	의견
20		Review	Review	Review
21		감각	크기	교통
22		움직임과 동작	안전과 사고	감정
23		미술	요일과 계절	제작과 판매
24		신체	자연 현상	동네와 길 찾기
25		Review	Review	Review
26		모양과 색깔	성격	행사와 시간
27		숫자	직업	능력
28		생활용품	얼굴과 인물 묘사	대중문화
29		직업	회사	필수 부사
30		Review	Review	Review
31		-ail, -ain	bl-, cl-, fl-, pl-	-ar-
32		-eat, -eed	cr-, dr-, fr-	-er
33	Phonics	-ight, -ind	sk-, sm-, sn-, sp-	-ir-
34		-one, -ore	kn-, -gn, -mb, wr-	-or-, -ur-
35		Review	Review	Review

Day 01~30

오늘 외운 단어를 내일은 몇 개나 기억할 수 있을까요?
하나의 주제와 연관된 단어들을 모아서
의미를 이해하며 외워 보세요.
단어들이 꼬리에 꼬리를 물고 연상되어
오래 기억할 수 있어요.
24가지 주제에 따라 구분된 480단어를
머릿속에 쏙쏙 넣어 보세요.

하나 더! 철저한 복습으로 잊혀져 가는 단어를
확실하게 내 것으로 만들어요.

01	**beef** [bi:f]	명 소고기 Cheese goes well with beef. 치즈는 소고기와 잘 어울린다.
02	**chicken** [tʃíkən]	명 닭고기, 닭 Paul loves to eat chicken soup. Paul은 닭고기 수프를 먹는 것을 정말 좋아한다.
03	**chocolate** [tʃɔ́:kəlit]	명 초콜릿 What is chocolate made from? 초콜릿은 무엇으로 만드니?
04	**coffee** [kɔ́(:)fi]	명 커피 Many people drink coffee here. 많은 사람들이 여기에서 커피를 마신다.
05	**curry** [kə́:ri]	명 카레 Why don't you add milk to the curry? 그 카레에 우유를 넣는 건 어때?
06	**fish** [fiʃ]	명 생선, 물고기　✿ 복수형 fish Fish go bad easily in hot weather. 생선은 더운 날씨에는 쉽게 상한다.
07	**hamburger** [hǽmbə̀ːrgər]	명 햄버거 My uncle doesn't like hamburgers. 나의 삼촌은 햄버거를 좋아하지 않는다.
08	**ice cream** [áiskri:m]	명 아이스크림 Ice cream will be served after dinner. 아이스크림은 저녁 식사 후에 제공될 것이다.
09	**noodles** [nú:dlz]	명 국수 Noodles are easy to cook. 국수는 요리하기 쉽다.
10	**pepper** [pépər]	명 후추 Does she need some pepper? 그녀는 후추가 필요하니?

A 우리말 뜻과 일치하도록 빠진 글자를 써넣어 단어를 완성하세요.

1 햄버거   h __ m __ __ r __ e __   2 소고기   __ __ __ f

3 후추   __ __ p __ e __   4 카레   __ u __ __ __

5 초콜릿   __ __ o __ __ l __ t __

B 다음 영어 단어의 우리말 뜻을 쓰세요.

1 fish   _______________   2 noodles   _______________

3 chicken   _______________   4 ice cream   _______________

5 coffee   _______________

C 우리말 뜻과 일치하도록 빈칸에 알맞은 단어를 써넣어 문장을 완성하세요.

1 Paul loves to eat _______________ soup.
Paul은 닭고기 수프를 먹는 것을 정말 좋아한다.

2 _______________ will be served after dinner.
아이스크림은 저녁 식사 후에 제공될 것이다.

3 What is _______________ made from?
초콜릿은 무엇으로 만드니?

4 _______________ go bad easily in hot weather.
생선은 더운 날씨에는 쉽게 상한다.

5 Cheese goes well with _______________.
치즈는 소고기와 잘 어울린다.

6 Why don't you add milk to the _______________?
그 카레에 우유를 넣는 건 어때?

7 Does she need some _______________?
그녀는 후추가 필요하니?

8 Many people drink _______________ here.
많은 사람들이 여기에서 커피를 마신다.

11	**pork** [pɔːrk]	명 돼지고기 Chop the pork and mix it with these carrots. 그 돼지고기를 다져서 이 당근과 섞어.
12	**rice** [rais]	명 쌀, 밥, 벼 They plant rice twice a year. 그들은 일 년에 두 번 벼를 심는다.
13	**salad** [sǽləd]	명 샐러드 Keep the salad in the refrigerator. 그 샐러드를 냉장고에 보관해.
14	**salt** [sɔːlt]	명 소금 Did you put salt into the onion soup? 너는 그 양파 수프에 소금을 넣었니?
15	**sandwich** [sǽndwitʃ]	명 샌드위치 Could you deliver these sandwiches? 이 샌드위치들을 배달해 주시겠어요?
16	**sauce** [sɔːs]	명 소스 I prepared hot sauce for him. 나는 그를 위해서 매운 소스를 준비했다.
17	**sausage** [sɔ́(ː)sidʒ]	명 소시지 We need four slices of sausage. 우리는 소시지 4조각이 필요하다.
18	**soda** [sóudə]	명 탄산음료 Will the kid order a can of soda? 그 아이는 탄산음료 한 캔을 주문할 거니?
19	**spaghetti** [spəɡéti]	명 스파게티 The spaghetti was tasty, wasn't it? 그 스파게티는 정말 맛있었어, 그렇지 않니?
20	**sugar** [ʃúɡər]	명 설탕 The cake contains too much sugar. 그 케이크에는 너무 많은 설탕이 들어 있다.

Daily Test

A 우리말 뜻과 일치하도록 빠진 글자를 써넣어 단어를 완성하세요.

1 소스   __ a __ c __

2 샐러드   __ __ __ a__

3 설탕   __ u __ __ __

4 돼지고기   p __ __ k

5 소시지   __ __ u __ a g __

B 다음 영어 단어의 우리말 뜻을 쓰세요.

1 rice   ________________

2 spaghetti   ________________

3 salt   ________________

4 soda   ________________

5 sandwich   ________________

C 우리말 뜻과 일치하도록 빈칸에 알맞은 단어를 써넣어 문장을 완성하세요.

1 Keep the ________________ in the refrigerator.
그 샐러드를 냉장고에 보관해.

2 We need four slices of ________________.
우리는 소시지 4조각이 필요하다.

3 Could you deliver these ________________?
이 샌드위치들을 배달해 주시겠어요?

4 Will the kid order a can of ________________?
그 아이는 탄산음료 한 캔을 주문할 거니?

5 Did you put ________________ into the onion soup?
너는 그 양파 수프에 소금을 넣었니?

6 The ________________ was tasty, wasn't it?
그 스파게티는 정말 맛있었어, 그렇지 않니?

7 I prepared hot ________________ for him.
나는 그를 위해서 매운 소스를 준비했다.

8 They plant ________________ twice a year.
그들은 일 년에 두 번 벼를 심는다.

01 alligator
[ǽləgèitər]

명 악어

Where do alligators mainly live?
악어들은 주로 어디에 사니?

02 blossom
[blásəm]

명 꽃　동 꽃을 피우다

The tree began to blossom.
그 나무는 꽃을 피우기 시작했다.

03 branch
[bræntʃ]

명 나뭇가지

Your hat was caught on a branch.
너의 모자가 나뭇가지에 걸렸다.

04 bud
[bʌd]

명 꽃봉오리, 싹

Look at those tulip buds!
저 튤립 봉오리들을 봐!

05 dolphin
[dálfin]

명 돌고래

How many teeth does a dolphin have?
돌고래는 이빨이 몇 개 있니?

06 goose
[gu:s]

명 거위　✿ 복수형 geese

A goose normally sits on eggs for 30 days.
거위는 보통 30일 동안 알을 품는다.

07 koala
[kouá:lə]

명 코알라

Don't touch the sleeping koala.
그 잠자는 코알라를 만지지 마.

08 mouse
[maus]

명 쥐　✿ 복수형 mice

The mouse came through the hole.
그 쥐는 그 구멍을 통해 들어왔다.

09 rabbit
[rǽbit]

명 토끼

The main character of the story is a rabbit.
그 이야기의 주인공은 토끼이다.

10 seal
[si:l]

명 물개, 바다표범

Did the seal hunt small fish?
그 물개는 작은 물고기들을 사냥했니?

Daily Test

A 우리말 뜻과 일치하도록 빠진 글자를 써넣어 단어를 완성하세요.

1 토끼 　　__ __ b __ i __ 　　**2** 코알라 　　__ __ __ l __

3 돌고래 　　d __ __ p __ __ n 　　**4** 나뭇가지 　　__ r __ __ c __

5 물개, 바다표범 　　__ __ a __

B 다음 영어 단어의 우리말 뜻을 쓰세요.

1 alligator 　　____________ 　　**2** goose 　　____________

3 blossom 　　____________ 　　**4** mouse 　　____________

5 bud 　　____________

C 우리말 뜻과 일치하도록 빈칸에 알맞은 단어를 써넣어 문장을 완성하세요.

1 The main character of the story is a ____________.
그 이야기의 주인공은 토끼이다.

2 Where do ____________ mainly live?
악어들은 주로 어디에 사니?

3 Don't touch the sleeping ____________.
그 잠자는 코알라를 만지지 마.

4 Your hat was caught on a ____________.
너의 모자가 나뭇가지에 걸렸다.

5 The tree began to ____________.
그 나무는 꽃을 피우기 시작했다.

6 The ____________ came through the hole.
그 쥐는 그 구멍을 통해 들어왔다.

7 Did the ____________ hunt small fish?
그 물개는 작은 물고기들을 사냥했니?

8 A ____________ normally sits on eggs for 30 days.
거위는 보통 30일 동안 알을 품는다.

11 seed
[siːd]
명 씨, 씨앗
You had better water the seeds every day.
너는 매일 그 씨앗들에 물을 주는 것이 좋겠다.

12 sheep
[ʃiːp]
명 양 ✿ 복수형 sheep
Can she take the sheep to the hill?
그녀는 그 양들을 언덕으로 데려갈 수 있니?

13 spider
[spáidər]
명 거미
A spider has eight legs.
거미는 다리가 여덟 개이다.

14 squirrel
[skwə́:rəl]
명 다람쥐
Why does a squirrel gather nuts?
다람쥐는 왜 견과류를 모으니?

15 stem
[stem]
명 줄기
The flower has a long stem.
그 꽃은 긴 줄기를 가지고 있다.

16 trunk
[trʌŋk]
명 나무의 몸통
A snake is crawling up the trunk.
뱀 한 마리가 그 나무의 몸통을 기어오르고 있다.

17 turtle
[tə́:rtl]
명 거북
My brother wants a turtle as a pet.
나의 남동생은 애완동물로 거북을 원한다.

18 weed
[wiːd]
명 잡초
The weeds didn't grow anymore.
그 잡초는 더 이상 자라지 않았다.

19 whale
[hweil]
명 고래
I actually saw a whale last week.
나는 지난주에 실제로 고래를 봤다.

20 wood
[wud]
명 나무, 목재
This wood chair is so comfortable.
이 나무 의자는 매우 편안하다.

Daily Test

A 우리말 뜻과 일치하도록 빠진 글자를 써넣어 단어를 완성하세요.

1 나무의 몸통   __ __ u n __   **2** 고래   w __ __ l __

3 양   __ __ e __ __   **4** 거북   __ u __ t __ __

5 씨, 씨앗   __ __ e __

B 다음 영어 단어의 우리말 뜻을 쓰세요.

1 stem   ___________________   **2** spider   ___________________

3 squirrel   ___________________   **4** weed   ___________________

5 wood   ___________________

C 우리말 뜻과 일치하도록 빈칸에 알맞은 단어를 써넣어 문장을 완성하세요.

1 The flower has a long ________________.
그 꽃은 긴 줄기를 가지고 있다.

2 A ________________ has eight legs.
거미는 다리가 여덟 개이다.

3 This ________________ chair is so comfortable.
이 나무 의자는 매우 편안하다.

4 Can she take the ________________ to the hill?
그녀는 그 양들을 언덕으로 데려갈 수 있니?

5 My brother wants a ________________ as a pet.
나의 남동생은 애완동물로 거북을 원한다.

6 You had better water the ________________ every day.
너는 매일 그 씨앗들에 물을 주는 것이 좋겠다.

7 Why does a ________________ gather nuts?
다람쥐는 왜 견과류를 모으니?

8 I actually saw a ________________ last week.
나는 지난주에 실제로 고래를 봤다.

01 abroad
[əbrɔ́:d]
(부) 해외로, 해외에
She is excited to go abroad this summer.
그녀는 이번 여름에 해외에 가게 되어 신이 나 있다.

02 baggage
[bǽgidʒ]
(명) 짐, 수하물
Check your baggage again before you leave.
떠나기 전에 너의 짐을 다시 확인해.

03 camping
[kǽmpiŋ]
(명) 캠핑, 야영
How was the camping in the forest?
숲에서 한 캠핑은 어땠니?

04 cancel
[kǽnsəl]
(동) 취소하다
They have to cancel the event.
그들은 그 행사를 취소해야 한다.

05 countryside
[kʌ́ntrisàid]
(명) 시골 지역
He drove to the countryside.
그는 시골 지역으로 운전해서 갔다.

06 fireworks
[fáiərwə:rks]
(명) 불꽃놀이
I can't wait to watch the fireworks.
나는 빨리 불꽃놀이를 보고 싶다.

07 hiking
[háikiŋ]
(명) 하이킹, 도보 여행
Which mountain is better for hiking?
어느 산이 하이킹에 더 좋니?

08 holiday
[hálidèi]
(명) 휴일, 휴가
What is the biggest holiday in America?
미국에서 가장 큰 휴일은 무엇이니?

09 hotel
[houtél]
(명) 호텔
Liz called the hotel to book a room.
Liz는 방을 예약하기 위해 호텔에 전화했다.

10 picnic
[píknik]
(명) 소풍　✿ go on a picnic 소풍을 가다
It is sunny, so they will go on a picnic.
날씨가 화창해서, 그들은 소풍을 갈 것이다.

Daily Test

A 우리말 뜻과 일치하도록 빠진 글자를 써넣어 단어를 완성하세요.

1 소풍   p __ __ n __ __　　　　2 캠핑, 야영   __ __ m __ __ __ g

3 취소하다   __ __ __ c __ l　　　　4 불꽃놀이   f __ __ __ w __ r __ s

5 하이킹, 도보 여행   __ __ __ __ n g

B 다음 영어 단어의 우리말 뜻을 쓰세요.

1 holiday　________________　　2 abroad　________________

3 countryside　________________　　4 baggage　________________

5 hotel　________________

C 우리말 뜻과 일치하도록 빈칸에 알맞은 단어를 써넣어 문장을 완성하세요.

1 He drove to the ________________.
그는 시골 지역으로 운전해서 갔다.

2 It is sunny, so they will go on a ________________.
날씨가 화창해서, 그들은 소풍을 갈 것이다.

3 Which mountain is better for ________________?
어느 산이 하이킹에 더 좋니?

4 Check your ________________ again before you leave.
떠나기 전에 너의 짐을 다시 확인해.

5 How was the ________________ in the forest?
숲에서 한 캠핑은 어땠니?

6 Liz called the ________________ to book a room.
Liz는 방을 예약하기 위해 호텔에 전화했다.

7 They have to ________________ the event.
그들은 그 행사를 취소해야 한다.

8 What is the biggest ________________ in America?
미국에서 가장 큰 휴일은 무엇이니?

11 plan
[plæn]

명 계획 동 계획을 세우다
I want to make a new plan.
나는 새로운 계획을 세우기를 원한다.

12 pool
[pu:l]

명 수영장
The indoor pool is for the students.
그 실내 수영장은 그 학생들을 위한 것이다.

13 sightseeing
[sáitsì:iŋ]

명 관광
I don't have enough time for sightseeing.
나는 관광할 충분한 시간이 없다.

14 sunglasses
[sʌ́nglæ̀siz]

명 선글라스
It is necessary to wear sunglasses.
선글라스를 쓸 필요가 있다.

15 swimsuit
[swímsjù:t]

명 수영복
Can you see Alice in a red swimsuit?
너는 빨간색 수영복을 입은 Alice가 보이니?

16 tent
[tent]

명 텐트, 천막
Let's set up a tent under this tree.
이 나무 아래에 텐트를 치자.

17 tourist
[tú(:)ərist]

명 관광객
Most tourists like to visit the Eiffel Tower.
관광객들 대부분은 에펠 탑을 방문하는 것을 좋아한다.

18 travel
[trǽvəl]

동 여행하다
He travels all over the world.
그는 전 세계를 여행한다.

19 trip
[trip]

명 여행
He is talking about his trip.
그는 그의 여행에 대해서 이야기하고 있다.

20 vacation
[veikéiʃən]

명 방학, 휴가
How long is your summer vacation?
너의 여름 방학은 얼마나 기니?

Daily Test

A 우리말 뜻과 일치하도록 빠진 글자를 써넣어 단어를 완성하세요.

1 여행　　　　　　 __ r __ __

2 선글라스　　　　 s __ __ g __ __ s s __ s

3 텐트, 천막　　　 t __ __ __

4 수영복　　　　　 __ __ __ m __ __ i t

5 계획; 계획을 세우다　 __ __ a __

B 다음 영어 단어의 우리말 뜻을 쓰세요.

1 travel　　　　　___________________

2 sightseeing　　___________________

3 tourist　　　　 ___________________

4 vacation　　　 ___________________

5 pool　　　　　 ___________________

C 우리말 뜻과 일치하도록 빈칸에 알맞은 단어를 써넣어 문장을 완성하세요.

1 Let's set up a ___________________ under this tree.
이 나무 아래에 텐트를 치자.

2 The indoor ___________________ is for the students.
그 실내 수영장은 그 학생들을 위한 것이다.

3 Most ___________________ like to visit the Eiffel Tower.
관광객들 대부분은 에펠 탑을 방문하는 것을 좋아한다.

4 How long is your summer ___________________?
너의 여름 방학은 얼마나 기니?

5 He is talking about his ___________________.
그는 그의 여행에 대해서 이야기하고 있다.

6 I want to make a new ___________________.
나는 새로운 계획을 세우기를 원한다.

7 He ___________________ all over the world.
그는 전 세계를 여행한다.

8 Can you see Alice in a red ___________________?
너는 빨간색 수영복을 입은 Alice가 보이니?

01 buy
[bai]

동 사다   ✿ buy-bought-bought
My sister never **buys** clothes on-line.
나의 언니는 절대 온라인으로 옷을 사지 않는다.

02 cart
[kɑːrt]

명 카트, 수레
Carts are near the entrance.
카트들은 입구 가까이에 있다.

03 cash
[kæʃ]

명 현금
How much **cash** do we need?
우리는 현금이 얼마나 필요하니?

04 cheap
[tʃiːp]

형 (값이) 싼
She found a **cheap** sofa at a retail store.
그녀는 소매점에서 싼 소파를 발견했다.

05 clerk
[kləːrk]

명 점원
He asks the **clerk** where coats are.
그는 그 점원에게 코트들이 어디에 있는지 묻는다.

06 coin
[kɔin]

명 동전
I took some **coins** out of my wallet.
나는 지갑에서 동전 몇 개를 꺼냈다.

07 cost
[kɔ(ː)st]

명 값, 비용   동 (값이) ~이다   ✿ cost-cost-cost
How much does the food **cost**?
그 음식은 얼마니?

08 credit card
[kréditkɑːrd]

명 신용 카드
What's wrong with my **credit card**?
나의 신용 카드에 무슨 문제가 있나요?

09 customer
[kʌstəmər]

명 손님, 고객
The **customer** sent a thank-you card.
그 고객은 감사 카드를 보냈다.

10 discount
[diskáunt]

명 할인   동 할인하다
They gave a 30% **discount** on the books.
그들은 그 책들에 대해 30% 할인을 해 주었다.

Daily Test

A 우리말 뜻과 일치하도록 빠진 글자를 써넣어 단어를 완성하세요.

1 카트, 수레   __ __ r __

2 동전   __ __ __ n

3 (값이) 싼   __ __ e __ __ __

4 현금   __ __ s __

5 손님, 고객   c __ __ t __ m __ __

B 다음 영어 단어의 우리말 뜻을 쓰세요.

1 clerk   _________________

2 credit card   _________________

3 buy   _________________

4 cost   _________________

5 discount   _________________

C 우리말 뜻과 일치하도록 빈칸에 알맞은 단어를 써넣어 문장을 완성하세요.

1 My sister never _________________ clothes on-line.
나의 언니는 절대 온라인으로 옷을 사지 않는다.

2 The _________________ sent a thank-you card.
그 고객은 감사 카드를 보냈다.

3 _________________ are near the entrance.
카트들은 입구 가까이에 있다.

4 What's wrong with my _________________?
나의 신용 카드에 무슨 문제가 있나요?

5 How much _________________ do we need?
우리는 현금이 얼마나 필요하니?

6 I took some _________________ out of my wallet.
나는 지갑에서 동전 몇 개를 꺼냈다.

7 She found a _________________ sofa at a retail store.
그녀는 소매점에서 싼 소파를 발견했다.

8 He asks the _________________ where coats are.
그는 그 점원에게 코트들이 어디에 있는지 묻는다.

11 display
[displéi]

동 진열하다　명 전시, 진열　✿ on display 진열된
Many flowers are on display at the store.
많은 꽃들이 가게에 진열되어 있다.

12 dollar
[dálər]

명 달러
The room is 100 dollars a night.
그 방은 하룻밤에 100달러이다.

13 expensive
[ikspénsiv]

형 비싼
Those shiny shoes look expensive.
저 반짝거리는 신발은 비싸 보인다.

14 grocery
[gróusəri]

명 식료품, 잡화
Philip is going to stop by the grocery store.
Philip은 그 식료품 가게에 들를 것이다.

15 pay
[pei]

동 (비용을) 지불하다　✿ pay-paid-paid
Did you pay for the yoga class?
너는 그 요가 수업에 비용을 지불했니?

16 receipt
[risí:t]

명 영수증
You don't have to get a receipt.
너희는 영수증을 받을 필요가 없다.

17 refund
[rí:fʌnd]

명 환불　동 환불하다
Where can I refund this bag?
어디에서 이 가방을 환불할 수 있나요?

18 save
[seiv]

동 저축하다, 절약하다
We are saving for a new house.
우리는 새 집을 위해 저축하고 있다.

19 shop
[ʃap]

명 가게　동 쇼핑하다
You can find a shoe shop around the corner.
너는 모퉁이를 돌면 신발 가게를 찾을 수 있다.

20 waste
[weist]

동 낭비하다　명 낭비
I must not waste my pocket money.
나는 나의 용돈을 낭비하면 안 된다.

A 우리말 뜻과 일치하도록 빠진 글자를 써넣어 단어를 완성하세요.

1 식료품, 잡화   __ r __ __ e __ y   **2** 저축하다, 절약하다   __ __ __ e

3 가게; 쇼핑하다   __ __ o __   **4** (비용을) 지불하다   __ __ y

5 달러   d __ __ l __ __

B 다음 영어 단어의 우리말 뜻을 쓰세요.

1 expensive   _________________   **2** display   _________________

3 waste   _________________   **4** refund   _________________

5 receipt   _________________

C 우리말 뜻과 일치하도록 빈칸에 알맞은 단어를 써넣어 문장을 완성하세요.

1 Did you _________________ for the yoga class?
너는 그 요가 수업에 비용을 지불했니?

2 Many flowers are on _________________ at the store.
많은 꽃들이 가게에 진열되어 있다.

3 I must not _________________ my pocket money.
나는 나의 용돈을 낭비하면 안 된다.

4 You can find a shoe _________________ around the corner.
너는 모퉁이를 돌면 신발 가게를 찾을 수 있다.

5 Philip is going to stop by the _________________ store.
Philip은 그 식료품 가게에 들를 것이다.

6 We are _________________ for a new house.
우리는 새 집을 위해 저축하고 있다.

7 Those shiny shoes look _________________.
저 반짝거리는 신발은 비싸 보인다.

8 Where can I _________________ this bag?
어디에서 이 가방을 환불할 수 있나요?

A 우리말 뜻에 해당하는 영어 단어를 찾아 동그라미 하세요.

| 줄기 | 소금 | 소풍 | 잡초 | 가게; 쇼핑하다 |
| 동전 | 탄산음료 | 여행하다 | 소고기 | 거위 |

g	p	w	c	p	j	s	k	l	p
b	e	e	f	i	m	a	z	q	r
d	s	e	m	c	h	l	m	n	t
g	w	d	l	n	s	t	e	m	r
c	o	i	n	i	h	h	t	j	a
q	y	o	b	c	o	j	v	d	v
n	g	t	s	h	p	k	o	z	e
v	f	x	r	e	c	s	t	m	l

B 우리말 뜻과 일치하도록 알맞은 단어를 골라 문장을 완성하세요.

| hamburgers | buds | plan | holiday | expensive | cost |

1 I want to make a new ________________.
나는 새로운 계획을 세우기를 원한다.

2 My uncle doesn't like ________________.
나의 삼촌은 햄버거를 좋아하지 않는다.

3 Those shiny shoes look ________________.
저 반짝거리는 신발은 비싸 보인다.

4 How much does the food ________________?
그 음식은 얼마니?

5 Look at those tulip ________________!
저 튤립 봉오리들을 봐!

6 What is the biggest ________________ in America?
미국에서 가장 큰 휴일은 무엇이니?

Day 05_C

C 들려 주는 영어 단어를 바르게 쓴 다음, 우리말 뜻을 써넣으세요.

	영어 단어	우리말		영어 단어	우리말
1			11		
2			12		
3			13		
4			14		
5			15		
6			16		
7			17		
8			18		
9			19		
10			20		

D 우리말 뜻과 일치하도록 알맞은 단어를 골라 동그라미 하세요.

1 Paul loves to eat (pepper / chicken) soup.
Paul은 닭고기 수프를 먹는 것을 정말 좋아한다.

2 Check your (baggage / trip) again before you leave.
떠나기 전에 너의 짐을 다시 확인해.

3 The (seal / mouse) came through the hole.
그 쥐는 그 구멍을 통해 들어왔다.

4 I prepared hot (sauce / sugar) for him.
나는 그를 위해서 매운 소스를 준비했다.

5 She found a (cheap / clerk) sofa at a retail store.
그녀는 소매점에서 싼 소파를 발견했다.

6 You had better water the (weeds / seeds) every day.
너는 매일 그 씨앗들에 물을 주는 것이 좋겠다.

 영어는 우리말로, 우리말은 영어로 바꿔 쓰세요.

1 cash ___________________

2 스파게티 ___________________

3 discount ___________________

4 취소하다 ___________________

5 turtle ___________________

6 아이스크림 ___________________

7 sandwich ___________________

8 관광 ___________________

9 wood ___________________

10 (비용을) 지불하다 ___________________

11 koala ___________________

12 방학, 휴가 ___________________

13 tourist ___________________

14 꽃; 꽃을 피우다 ___________________

15 waste ___________________

16 양 ___________________

17 hiking ___________________

18 커피 ___________________

19 rice ___________________

20 점원 ___________________

Day 05_F

 잘 듣고, 빈칸에 알맞은 단어를 써넣어 문장을 완성하세요.

1 Did the ___________________ hunt small fish?

2 Why don't you add milk to the ___________________?

3 She is excited to go ___________________ this summer.

4 A snake is crawling up the ___________________.

5 The ___________________ sent a thank-you card.

6 Chop the ___________________ and mix it with these carrots.

7 Can you see Alice in a red ___________________?

8 Philip is going to stop by the ___________________ store.

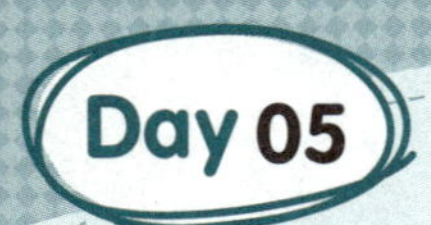

Day 05

 우리말 뜻과 일치하도록 빈칸에 알맞은 단어를 써넣어 문장을 완성하세요.

1 My sister never b________________ clothes on-line.
나의 언니는 절대 온라인으로 옷을 사지 않는다.

2 What is c________________ made from?
초콜릿은 무엇으로 만드니?

3 He drove to the c________________.
그는 시골 지역으로 운전해서 갔다.

4 It is necessary to wear s________________.
선글라스를 쓸 필요가 있다.

5 How many teeth does a d________________ have?
돌고래는 이빨이 몇 개 있니?

6 You don't have to get a r________________.
너희는 영수증을 받을 필요가 없다.

7 The cake contains too much s________________.
그 케이크에는 너무 많은 설탕이 들어 있다.

8 Liz called the h________________ to book a room.
Liz는 방을 예약하기 위해 호텔에 전화했다.

9 Why does a s________________ gather nuts?
다람쥐는 왜 견과류를 모으니?

10 Where can I r________________ this bag?
어디에서 이 가방을 환불할 수 있나요?

Review에서 틀린 문제의 영어 단어와 우리말 뜻을 쓴 다음, 영어 단어를 3번씩 쓰세요.

	( )	________ ________ ________
	( )	________ ________ ________
	( )	________ ________ ________
	( )	________ ________ ________
	( )	________ ________ ________

Day 06 장소

01 airport
[ɛ́ərpɔ̀ːrt]

명 공항

How can I get to the airport?
공항에 어떻게 갈 수 있나요?

02 aquarium
[əkwɛ́(ː)əriəm]

명 수족관

The aquarium is open to students for free.
그 수족관은 학생들에게 무료로 개방된다.

03 bakery
[béikəri]

명 빵집, 제과점

The bakery is famous for apple pies.
그 빵집은 사과 파이로 유명하다.

04 bank
[bæŋk]

명 은행

Turn left, and you can see the bank.
왼쪽으로 돌아, 그러면 그 은행을 볼 수 있어.

05 bookstore
[búkstɔ̀ːr]

명 서점

The bookstore sells only guidebooks.
그 서점은 여행 안내서만 판다.

06 church
[tʃəːrtʃ]

명 교회

The church was built 200 years ago.
그 교회는 200년 전에 지어졌다.

07 drugstore
[drʌ́gstɔ̀ːr]

명 약국

The drugstore closes at 10 p.m.
그 약국은 오후 10시에 문을 닫는다.

08 farm
[fɑːrm]

명 농장

Is there a farm near the stream?
개울 근처에 농장이 하나 있니?

09 fire station
[fáiərstèiʃən]

명 소방서

They will visit the fire station this Friday.
그들은 이번 주 금요일에 그 소방서를 방문할 것이다.

10 harbor
[hɑ́ːrbər]

명 항구

She can see the harbor from her room.
그녀는 그녀의 방에서 그 항구를 볼 수 있다.

Daily Test

A 우리말 뜻과 일치하도록 빠진 글자를 써넣어 단어를 완성하세요.

1 빵집, 제과점   __ a __ __ r __

2 농장   __ __ r __

3 항구   __ __ r __ o __

4 수족관   __ q __ __ r __ __ m

5 교회   c __ __ __ c h

B 다음 영어 단어의 우리말 뜻을 쓰세요.

1 bank   _________________

2 fire station   _________________

3 airport   _________________

4 bookstore   _________________

5 drugstore   _________________

C 우리말 뜻과 일치하도록 빈칸에 알맞은 단어를 써넣어 문장을 완성하세요.

1 The _________________ was built 200 years ago.
그 교회는 200년 전에 지어졌다.

2 She can see the _________________ from her room.
그녀는 그녀의 방에서 그 항구를 볼 수 있다.

3 Turn left, and you can see the _________________.
왼쪽으로 돌아, 그러면 그 은행을 볼 수 있어.

4 The _________________ is open to students for free.
그 수족관은 학생들에게 무료로 개방된다.

5 The _________________ sells only guidebooks.
그 서점은 여행 안내서만 판다.

6 They will visit the _________________ this Friday.
그들은 이번 주 금요일에 그 소방서를 방문할 것이다.

7 The _________________ closes at 10 p.m.
그 약국은 오후 10시에 문을 닫는다.

8 The _________________ is famous for apple pies.
그 빵집은 사과 파이로 유명하다.

Day 06　장소

11 hospital
[háspitəl]

명 병원
An ambulance took them to the hospital.
구급차가 그들을 병원으로 데려갔다.

12 market
[máːrkit]

명 시장
The market was crowded with people.
그 시장은 사람들로 붐볐다.

13 museum
[mju(ː)zí(ː)əm]

명 박물관, 미술관
She works for a museum.
그녀는 박물관에서 일한다.

14 park
[pɑːrk]

명 공원
Cars are not allowed in this park.
이 공원에서 차는 허용되지 않는다.

15 police station
[pəlíːsstèiʃən]

명 경찰서
How far is the police station from here?
경찰서는 여기에서 얼마나 머니?

16 post office
[póustɔ̀(ː)fis]

명 우체국
We will send the letters at the post office.
우리는 우체국에서 그 편지들을 보낼 것이다.

17 restaurant
[réstərənt]

명 식당
This restaurant serves Korean food.
이 식당은 한국 음식을 제공한다.

18 school
[skuːl]

명 학교
The school is in the center of the village.
그 학교는 마을의 중앙에 있다.

19 stadium
[stéidiəm]

명 경기장, 스타디움
The fans waited in front of the stadium.
그 팬들은 경기장 앞에서 기다렸다.

20 theater
[θí(ː)ətər]

명 극장
A few theaters show the movie.
몇몇 극장들이 그 영화를 상영한다.

Daily Test

A 우리말 뜻과 일치하도록 빠진 글자를 써넣어 단어를 완성하세요.

1 박물관, 미술관   _ _ s e _ _

2 병원   _ _ s p _ t _ _

3 공원   _ _ r _

4 학교   _ _ h o _ _

5 경기장, 스타디움   s _ _ _ i _ m

B 다음 영어 단어의 우리말 뜻을 쓰세요.

1 post office __________________

2 theater __________________

3 market __________________

4 restaurant __________________

5 police station __________________

C 우리말 뜻과 일치하도록 빈칸에 알맞은 단어를 써넣어 문장을 완성하세요.

1 An ambulance took them to the ________________.
구급차가 그들을 병원으로 데려갔다.

2 How far is the ________________ from here?
경찰서는 여기에서 얼마나 머니?

3 The fans waited in front of the ________________.
그 팬들은 경기장 앞에서 기다렸다.

4 This ________________ serves Korean food.
이 식당은 한국 음식을 제공한다.

5 We will send the letters at the ________________.
우리는 우체국에서 그 편지들을 보낼 것이다.

6 The ________________ is in the center of the village.
그 학교는 마을의 중앙에 있다.

7 Cars are not allowed in this ________________.
이 공원에서 차는 허용되지 않는다.

8 The ________________ was crowded with people.
그 시장은 사람들로 붐볐다.

01 admire
[ədmáiər]

동 존경하다, 칭찬하다

I admire your courage.
나는 너의 용기를 존경한다.

02 alone
[əlóun]

형 혼자인 부 혼자

She sometimes spends time alone.
그녀는 가끔 혼자 시간을 보낸다.

03 apology
[əpálədʒi]

명 사과

Will he accept Kathy's apology?
그가 Kathy의 사과를 받아 줄까?

04 appointment
[əpɔ́intmənt]

명 약속 ✿ make an appointment 약속을 잡다

She made an appointment with a doctor.
그녀는 의사와 약속을 잡았다.

05 behavior
[bihéivjər]

명 행동

His behavior made his mom happy.
그의 행동은 그의 엄마를 행복하게 했다.

06 bow
[bau]

동 (고개 숙여) 인사하다

The magician bowed to the people.
그 마술사는 사람들에게 고개 숙여 인사했다.

07 fair
[fɛər]

형 공정한

The teacher's decision was fair.
그 선생님의 결정은 공정했다.

08 familiar
[fəmíljər]

형 익숙한, 친숙한 ✿ familiar to ~에게 친숙한

Her voice is familiar to the baby.
그녀의 목소리는 그 아기에게 친숙하다.

09 fault
[fɔːlt]

명 잘못

Do you think it is his fault?
너는 그것이 그의 잘못이라고 생각하니?

10 favor
[féivər]

명 호의, 부탁 ✿ do ~ a favor ~의 부탁을 들어주다

Will you do me a favor?
내 부탁 하나만 들어줄래?

Daily Test

A 우리말 뜻과 일치하도록 빠진 글자를 써넣어 단어를 완성하세요.

1 공정한   __ __ __ r

2 혼자인; 혼자   __ l __ n __

3 (고개 숙여) 인사하다   __ o __

4 사과   a __ __ l __ __ y

5 잘못   __ a __ __ __

B 다음 영어 단어의 우리말 뜻을 쓰세요.

1 admire   __________________

2 favor   __________________

3 familiar   __________________

4 behavior   __________________

5 appointment   __________________

C 우리말 뜻과 일치하도록 빈칸에 알맞은 단어를 써넣어 문장을 완성하세요.

1 The magician __________________ to the people.
그 마술사는 사람들에게 고개 숙여 인사했다.

2 She sometimes spends time __________________.
그녀는 가끔 혼자 시간을 보낸다.

3 I __________________ your courage.
나는 너의 용기를 존경한다.

4 Do you think it is his __________________?
너는 그것이 그의 잘못이라고 생각하니?

5 The teacher's decision was __________________.
그 선생님의 결정은 공정했다.

6 Will he accept Kathy's __________________?
그가 Kathy의 사과를 받아 줄까?

7 His __________________ made his mom happy.
그의 행동은 그의 엄마를 행복하게 했다.

8 Her voice is __________________ to the baby.
그녀의 목소리는 그 아기에게 친숙하다.

11 friend
[frend]

명 친구
Did Bob have fun with his friends?
Bob은 그의 친구들과 즐거운 시간을 보냈니?

12 friendship
[fréndʃip]

명 우정
Your friendship means a lot to me.
너의 우정은 나에게 큰 의미가 있다.

13 greet
[griːt]

동 환영하다
Everyone greeted us gladly.
모든 사람이 우리를 기쁘게 환영했다.

14 help
[help]

동 도와주다 명 도움
We must help each other.
우리는 서로를 도와야 한다.

15 hug
[hʌg]

동 껴안다
The kid hugged the teddy bear.
그 아이는 그 곰 인형을 껴안았다.

16 introduce
[ìntrədjúːs]

동 소개하다
Let me introduce myself.
제 소개를 하겠습니다.

17 partner
[páːrtnər]

명 파트너, 동업자
My partner and I worked late yesterday.
나의 동업자와 나는 어제 늦게까지 일했다.

18 refuse
[rifjúːz]

동 거절하다
The pianist refused to play the piano.
그 피아니스트는 피아노 연주하기를 거절했다.

19 share
[ʃɛər]

동 함께 쓰다, 나누다
He shares the room with his brother.
그는 그의 형과 방을 함께 쓴다.

20 thank
[θæŋk]

동 고마워하다
Thank you for inviting me.
나를 초대해줘서 고마워.

A 우리말 뜻과 일치하도록 빠진 글자를 써넣어 단어를 완성하세요.

1 환영하다   __ r __ e __   2 파트너, 동업자   __ a __ __ n __ r

3 도와주다; 도움   __ __ __ p   4 함께 쓰다, 나누다   s __ __ r __

5 친구   __ __ i __ __ d

B 다음 영어 단어의 우리말 뜻을 쓰세요.

1 hug   _________________   2 thank   _________________

3 friendship   _________________   4 refuse   _________________

5 introduce   _________________

C 우리말 뜻과 일치하도록 빈칸에 알맞은 단어를 써넣어 문장을 완성하세요.

1 Your _________________ means a lot to me.
너의 우정은 나에게 큰 의미가 있다.

2 The kid _________________ the teddy bear.
그 아이는 그 곰 인형을 껴안았다.

3 _________________ you for inviting me.
나를 초대해줘서 고마워.

4 Let me _________________ myself.
제 소개를 하겠습니다.

5 Did Bob have fun with his _________________?
Bob은 그의 친구들과 즐거운 시간을 보냈니?

6 We must _________________ each other.
우리는 서로를 도와야 한다.

7 Everyone _________________ us gladly.
모든 사람이 우리를 기쁘게 환영했다.

8 He _________________ the room with his brother.
그는 그의 형과 방을 함께 쓴다.

01 absent
[ǽbsənt]

형 결석한　✿ absent from ~에 결석한
Why was she absent from school?
그녀는 왜 학교에 결석했니?

02 art room
[áːrtrù(ː)m]

명 미술실
They cleaned the art room together.
그들은 함께 그 미술실을 청소했다.

03 attend
[əténd]

동 참석하다, 다니다
We attend the same school.
우리는 같은 학교에 다닌다.

04 cafeteria
[kæ̀fətíəriə]

명 구내식당, 카페테리아
He is eating in the cafeteria.
그는 구내식당에서 먹고 있다.

05 classmate
[klǽsmèit]

명 반 친구
I played tennis with my classmate.
나는 나의 반 친구와 테니스를 쳤다.

06 classroom
[klǽsrù(ː)m]

명 교실
Look at the board in the classroom.
교실에 있는 칠판을 봐.

07 club
[klʌb]

명 클럽, 동호회
Our club needs new members.
우리 동호회는 새로운 회원이 필요하다.

08 exam
[igzǽm]

명 시험
I have an important exam in the afternoon.
나는 오후에 중요한 시험이 있다.

09 grade
[greid]

명 성적, 학년
We are in the sixth grade.
우리는 6학년이다.

10 graduate
[grǽdʒuèit]

동 졸업하다
I will graduate next year.
나는 내년에 졸업할 것이다.

Daily Test

A 우리말 뜻과 일치하도록 빠진 글자를 써넣어 단어를 완성하세요.

1 클럽, 동호회   __ __ u __

2 성적, 학년   g __ __ d __

3 졸업하다   __ r __ d __ __ __ __

4 참석하다, 다니다   __ __ t e __ __

5 결석한   a __ __ __ n __

B 다음 영어 단어의 우리말 뜻을 쓰세요.

1 art room   _______________

2 classmate   _______________

3 exam   _______________

4 cafeteria   _______________

5 classroom   _______________

C 우리말 뜻과 일치하도록 빈칸에 알맞은 단어를 써넣어 문장을 완성하세요.

1 I will _______________ next year.
나는 내년에 졸업할 것이다.

2 I played tennis with my _______________.
나는 나의 반 친구와 테니스를 쳤다.

3 He is eating in the _______________.
그는 구내식당에서 먹고 있다.

4 Our _______________ needs new members.
우리 동호회는 새로운 회원이 필요하다.

5 They cleaned the _______________ together.
그들은 함께 그 미술실을 청소했다.

6 We are in the sixth _______________.
우리는 6학년이다.

7 Look at the board in the _______________.
교실에 있는 칠판을 봐.

8 Why was she _______________ from school?
그녀는 왜 학교에 결석했니?

11 gym
[dʒim]
명 체육관
They are practicing in the gym.
그들은 체육관에서 연습하고 있다.

12 join
[dʒɔin]
동 가입하다
Sam wants to join the band.
Sam은 그 밴드에 가입하고 싶어 한다.

13 library
[láibrèri]
명 도서관
The light is on in the library.
도서관에 불이 켜져 있다.

14 music room
[mjú:zikrù(:)m]
명 음악실
The music room has two doors.
그 음악실에는 문이 2개 있다.

15 playground
[pléigràund]
명 운동장, 놀이터
Let's make a snowman in the playground.
운동장에서 눈사람을 만들자.

16 principal
[prínsəpəl]
명 교장, 총장
I met the principal on the way home.
나는 집에 가는 길에 교장 선생님을 만났다.

17 semester
[siméstər]
명 학기
The spring semester starts tomorrow.
봄 학기는 내일 시작된다.

18 study
[stʌdi]
동 공부하다
My father studied law at university.
나의 아버지는 대학에서 법을 공부하셨다.

19 timetable
[táimtèibl]
명 시간표
We got a new timetable this morning.
우리는 오늘 아침에 새로운 시간표를 받았다.

20 uniform
[jú:nəfɔ̀:rm]
명 교복, 유니폼
You don't have to wear uniforms on Fridays.
너희는 금요일에 교복을 입을 필요가 없다.

Daily Test

A 우리말 뜻과 일치하도록 빠진 글자를 써넣어 단어를 완성하세요.

1 가입하다   __ o __ __

2 시간표   t __ m __ __ a __ __ e

3 체육관   __ __ m

4 교복, 유니폼   __ n __ __ o __ __

5 공부하다   __ t __ d __

B 다음 영어 단어의 우리말 뜻을 쓰세요.

1 principal   _______________

2 library   _______________

3 playground   _______________

4 music room   _______________

5 semester   _______________

C 우리말 뜻과 일치하도록 빈칸에 알맞은 단어를 써넣어 문장을 완성하세요.

1 I met the _______________ on the way home.
나는 집에 가는 길에 교장 선생님을 만났다.

2 Sam wants to _______________ the band.
Sam은 그 밴드에 가입하고 싶어 한다.

3 They are practicing in the _______________.
그들은 체육관에서 연습하고 있다.

4 Let's make a snowman in the _______________.
운동장에서 눈사람을 만들자.

5 The spring _______________ starts tomorrow.
봄 학기는 내일 시작된다.

6 My father _______________ law at university.
나의 아버지는 대학에서 법을 공부하셨다.

7 The light is on in the _______________.
도서관에 불이 켜져 있다.

8 We got a new _______________ this morning.
우리는 오늘 아침에 새로운 시간표를 받았다.

Day 09 — 나라와 지역

01 Africa
[ǽfrikə]
명 아프리카
They left for Africa a week ago.
그들은 일주일 전에 아프리카로 떠났다.

02 America
[əmérikə]
명 미국, 아메리카 대륙
The sisters grew up in America.
그 자매들은 미국에서 자랐다.

03 Asia
[éiʒə]
명 아시아
They were the first Olympic Games in Asia.
그것은 아시아에서 열린 첫 번째 올림픽 대회였다.

04 Australia
[ɔ(:)stréiljə]
명 호주
How long will you stay in Australia?
너는 호주에 얼마나 오래 머무를 거니?

05 Canada
[kǽnədə]
명 캐나다
Ottawa is the capital of Canada.
오타와는 캐나다의 수도이다.

06 China
[tʃáinə]
명 중국
I will study in China next month.
나는 다음 달에 중국에서 공부할 것이다.

07 continent
[kántənənt]
명 대륙
There are seven continents in the world.
세계에는 7개의 대륙이 있다.

08 country
[kʌ́ntri]
명 국가, 나라
It's snowing all over the country.
전국적으로 눈이 내리고 있다.

09 England
[íŋɡlənd]
명 영국
He arrived in England last night.
그는 어젯밤에 영국에 도착했다.

10 Europe
[júːərəp]
명 유럽
We started preparing for a trip to Europe.
우리는 유럽 여행 준비를 시작했다.

Daily Test

A 우리말 뜻과 일치하도록 빠진 글자를 써넣어 단어를 완성하세요.

1 캐나다   _ _ n a _ _

2 아프리카   A _ _ i c _

3 유럽   E u _ _ _ _

4 아시아   _ s i _

5 국가, 나라   _ _ _ n _ _ y

B 다음 영어 단어의 우리말 뜻을 쓰세요.

1 China _______________

2 England _______________

3 America _______________

4 continent _______________

5 Australia _______________

C 우리말 뜻과 일치하도록 빈칸에 알맞은 단어를 써넣어 문장을 완성하세요.

1 They left for _______________ a week ago.
그들은 일주일 전에 아프리카로 떠났다.

2 I will study in _______________ next month.
나는 다음 달에 중국에서 공부할 것이다.

3 There are seven _______________ in the world.
세계에는 7개의 대륙이 있다.

4 How long will you stay in _______________?
너는 호주에 얼마나 오래 머무를 거니?

5 The sisters grew up in _______________.
그 자매들은 미국에서 자랐다.

6 He arrived in _______________ last night.
그는 어젯밤에 영국에 도착했다.

7 They were the first Olympic Games in _______________.
그것은 아시아에서 열린 첫 번째 올림픽 대회였다.

8 Ottawa is the capital of _______________.
오타와는 캐나다의 수도이다.

11 France
[fræns]

명 프랑스

I got a call from Mr. Smith in France.
나는 프랑스에 있는 Smith 씨에게서 온 전화를 받았다.

12 Italy
[ítəli]

명 이탈리아

Italy looks like a boot, doesn't it?
이탈리아는 장화처럼 생겼어, 그렇지 않니?

13 Japan
[dʒəpǽn]

명 일본

My cousin works in Japan as a doctor.
나의 사촌은 일본에서 의사로 일한다.

14 Korea
[kərí(:)ə]

명 한국

The artist will come back to Korea soon.
그 화가는 곧 한국에 돌아올 것이다.

15 land
[lænd]

명 육지, 땅

Sea turtles lay eggs on land.
바다거북은 육지에서 알을 낳는다.

16 national
[nǽʃənəl]

형 국가의

He will join the national team.
그는 국가 대표팀에 합류할 것이다.

17 ocean
[óuʃən]

명 대양, 바다

The ship is sailing across the ocean.
그 배는 바다를 가로질러 항해하고 있다.

18 region
[ríːdʒən]

명 지역

It is hard to grow plants in this region.
이 지역에서 식물을 기르는 것은 힘들다.

19 Russia
[rʌ́ʃə]

명 러시아

Russia has the deepest lake in the world.
러시아에는 세계에서 가장 깊은 호수가 있다.

20 Spain
[spein]

명 스페인

Many people in Spain love soccer.
스페인에 있는 많은 사람들이 축구를 사랑한다.

A 우리말 뜻과 일치하도록 빠진 글자를 써넣어 단어를 완성하세요.

1 한국   __ __ __ e __   2 이탈리아   __ t __ l __

3 대양, 바다   o __ __ a __   4 러시아   __ __ s __ __ a

5 육지, 땅   __ __ __ d

B 다음 영어 단어의 우리말 뜻을 쓰세요.

1 national   __________________   2 France   __________________

3 Spain   __________________   4 Japan   __________________

5 region   __________________

C 우리말 뜻과 일치하도록 빈칸에 알맞은 단어를 써넣어 문장을 완성하세요.

1 Sea turtles lay eggs on ________________.
바다거북은 육지에서 알을 낳는다.

2 ________________ looks like a boot, doesn't it?
이탈리아는 장화처럼 생겼어, 그렇지 않니?

3 I got a call from Mr. Smith in ________________.
나는 프랑스에 있는 Smith 씨에게서 온 전화를 받았다.

4 It is hard to grow plants in this ________________.
이 지역에서 식물을 기르는 것은 힘들다.

5 Many people in ________________ love soccer.
스페인에 있는 많은 사람들이 축구를 사랑한다.

6 My cousin works in ________________ as a doctor.
나의 사촌은 일본에서 의사로 일한다.

7 ________________ has the deepest lake in the world.
러시아에는 세계에서 가장 깊은 호수가 있다.

8 The artist will come back to ________________ soon.
그 화가는 곧 한국에 돌아올 것이다.

A 우리말 뜻에 해당하는 영어 단어를 찾아 동그라미 하세요.

중국	항구	혼자인; 혼자	은행	성적, 학년
공정한	환영하다	공부하다	육지, 땅	가입하다

z	v	w	v	h	j	m	q	p	g
f	a	i	r	z	a	o	d	s	r
l	h	h	v	l	l	r	i	v	e
y	b	p	n	a	o	b	b	n	e
b	q	c	d	n	n	f	w	o	t
a	g	r	a	d	e	x	g	v	r
n	h	w	s	t	u	d	y	f	g
k	t	k	j	m	C	h	i	n	a

B 우리말 뜻과 일치하도록 알맞은 단어를 골라 문장을 완성하세요.

national	attend	theaters	Europe	farm	favor

1 We _________________ the same school.
우리는 같은 학교에 다닌다.

2 Will you do me a _________________?
내 부탁 하나만 들어줄래?

3 He will join the _________________ team.
그는 국가 대표팀에 합류할 것이다.

4 A few _________________ show the movie.
몇몇 극장들이 그 영화를 상영한다.

5 We started preparing for a trip to _________________.
우리는 유럽 여행 준비를 시작했다.

6 Is there a _________________ near the stream?
개울 근처에 농장이 하나 있니?

C 들려 주는 영어 단어를 바르게 쓴 다음, 우리말 뜻을 써넣으세요.

Day 10_C

	영어 단어	우리말		영어 단어	우리말
1			11		
2			12		
3			13		
4			14		
5			15		
6			16		
7			17		
8			18		
9			19		
10			20		

D 우리말 뜻과 일치하도록 알맞은 단어를 골라 동그라미 하세요.

1 I have an important (grade / exam) in the afternoon.
   나는 오후에 중요한 시험이 있다.

2 She made an (apology / appointment) with a doctor.
   그녀는 의사와 약속을 잡았다.

3 You don't have to wear (uniforms / principals) on Fridays.
   너희는 금요일에 교복을 입을 필요가 없다.

4 How can I get to the (bookstore / airport)?
   공항에 어떻게 갈 수 있나요?

5 My (friend / partner) and I worked late yesterday.
   나의 동업자와 나는 어제 늦게까지 일했다.

6 The ship is sailing across the (ocean / region).
   그 배는 바다를 가로질러 항해하고 있다.

E 영어는 우리말로, 우리말은 영어로 바꿔 쓰세요.

1	help ___________	2	아프리카 ___________
3	familiar ___________	4	식당 ___________
5	art room ___________	6	소개하다 ___________
7	Asia ___________	8	교실 ___________
9	drugstore ___________	10	운동장, 놀이터 ___________
11	France ___________	12	학교 ___________
13	library ___________	14	한국 ___________
15	behavior ___________	16	졸업하다 ___________
17	hospital ___________	18	캐나다 ___________
19	Spain ___________	20	경찰서 ___________

F 잘 듣고, 빈칸에 알맞은 단어를 써넣어 문장을 완성하세요.

Day 10_F

1 I played tennis with my ___________.

2 Do you think it is his ___________?

3 It's snowing all over the ___________.

4 The ___________ sells only guidebooks.

5 ___________ looks like a boot, doesn't it?

6 She works for a ___________.

7 The spring ___________ starts tomorrow.

8 The pianist ___________ to play the piano.

G 우리말 뜻과 일치하도록 빈칸에 알맞은 단어를 써넣어 문장을 완성하세요.

1 The m________________ was crowded with people.
그 시장은 사람들로 붐볐다.

2 I met the p________________ on the way home.
나는 집에 가는 길에 교장 선생님을 만났다.

3 I a________________ your courage.
나는 너의 용기를 존경한다.

4 He s________________ the room with his brother.
그는 그의 형과 방을 함께 쓴다.

5 The a________________ is open to students for free.
그 수족관은 학생들에게 무료로 개방된다.

6 There are seven c________________ in the world.
세계에는 7개의 대륙이 있다.

7 Why was she a________________ from school?
그녀는 왜 학교에 결석했니?

8 The fans waited in front of the s________________.
그 팬들은 경기장 앞에서 기다렸다.

9 Your f________________ means a lot to me.
너의 우정은 나에게 큰 의미가 있다.

10 It is hard to grow plants in this r________________.
이 지역에서 식물을 기르는 것은 힘들다.

✎ Review에서 틀린 문제의 영어 단어와 우리말 뜻을 쓴 다음, 영어 단어를 3번씩 쓰세요.

	( )	________ ________ ________
	( )	________ ________ ________
	( )	________ ________ ________
	( )	________ ________ ________
	( )	________ ________ ________

Day 11_01

01 first
[fəːrst]

형 첫 번째의, 제1의
Today is your first day at school.
오늘은 네가 학교에 가는 첫 번째 날이다.

02 second
[sékənd]

형 두 번째의, 제2의
It will be her second visit to Busan.
그것은 그녀의 두 번째 부산 방문이 될 것이다.

03 third
[θəːrd]

형 세 번째의, 제3의
Third grade students learn English.
3학년 학생들은 영어를 배운다.

04 fourth
[fɔːrθ]

형 네 번째의, 제4의
It is the fourth book of the series.
그것은 그 시리즈의 네 번째 책이다.

05 fifth
[fifθ]

형 다섯 번째의, 제5의
This is her fifth award for the movie.
이것은 그녀가 그 영화로 받은 다섯 번째 상이다.

06 sixth
[siksθ]

형 여섯 번째의, 제6의
She is the sixth tallest kid in the class.
그녀는 그 반에서 여섯 번째로 키가 큰 아이이다.

07 seventh
[sévənθ]

형 일곱 번째의, 제7의
I set a new record on my seventh try.
나는 일곱 번째 시도에서 신기록을 세웠다.

08 eighth
[eitθ]

형 여덟 번째의, 제8의
Tom drew the eighth house.
Tom은 여덟 번째 집을 그렸다.

09 ninth
[nainθ]

형 아홉 번째의, 제9의
Please read the ninth sentence.
아홉 번째 문장을 읽어 주세요.

10 tenth
[tenθ]

형 열 번째의, 제10의
The runner took tenth place.
그 주자는 10등을 차지했다.

Daily Test

A 우리말 뜻과 일치하도록 빠진 글자를 써넣어 단어를 완성하세요.

1 세 번째의   __ __ i __ __

2 첫 번째의   __ i __ __ __

3 아홉 번째의   __ i __ __ __

4 다섯 번째의   __ __ f __ __

5 여덟 번째의   e __ g __ __ __

B 다음 영어 단어의 우리말 뜻을 쓰세요.

1 sixth   _________________

2 tenth   _________________

3 second   _________________

4 fourth   _________________

5 seventh   _________________

C 우리말 뜻과 일치하도록 빈칸에 알맞은 단어를 써넣어 문장을 완성하세요.

1 Today is your _________________ day at school.
오늘은 네가 학교에 가는 첫 번째 날이다.

2 Tom drew the _________________ house.
Tom은 여덟 번째 집을 그렸다.

3 I set a new record on my _________________ try.
나는 일곱 번째 시도에서 신기록을 세웠다.

4 It is the _________________ book of the series.
그것은 그 시리즈의 네 번째 책이다.

5 It will be her _________________ visit to Busan.
그것은 그녀의 두 번째 부산 방문이 될 것이다.

6 Please read the _________________ sentence.
아홉 번째 문장을 읽어 주세요.

7 She is the _________________ tallest kid in the class.
그녀는 그 반에서 여섯 번째로 키가 큰 아이이다.

8 This is her _________________ award for the movie.
이것은 그녀가 그 영화로 받은 다섯 번째 상이다.

11 eleventh
[ilévənθ]
형 열한 번째의, 제11의
It's time to answer the eleventh question.
열한 번째 질문에 대답할 시간이다.

12 twelfth
[twelfθ]
형 열두 번째의, 제12의
My twelfth birthday was a month ago.
나의 열두 번째 생일은 한 달 전이었다.

13 thirteenth
[θə̀:rtí:nθ]
형 열세 번째의, 제13의
How much is the thirteenth umbrella?
열세 번째 우산은 얼마인가요?

14 fourteenth
[fɔ̀:rtí:nθ]
형 열네 번째의, 제14의
He hides the gift in the fourteenth box.
그는 그 선물을 열네 번째 상자에 숨긴다.

15 fifteenth
[fìftí:nθ]
형 열다섯 번째의, 제15의
I received the fifteenth call.
나는 열다섯 번째 전화를 받았다.

16 sixteenth
[sìkstí:nθ]
형 열여섯 번째의, 제16의
The sixteenth design is great.
열여섯 번째 디자인이 훌륭하다.

17 seventeenth
[sèvəntí:nθ]
형 열일곱 번째의, 제17의
They sat in the seventeenth row.
그들은 열일곱 번째 줄에 앉았다.

18 eighteenth
[èití:nθ]
형 열여덟 번째의, 제18의
The eighteenth boy raised his hand.
열여덟 번째 소년이 손을 들었다.

19 nineteenth
[nàintí:nθ]
형 열아홉 번째의, 제19의
Is the nineteenth player kicking a ball?
열아홉 번째 선수가 공을 차고 있니?

20 twentieth
[twéntiiθ]
형 스무 번째의, 제20의
We were working on the twentieth floor.
우리는 20층에서 일을 하고 있었다.

Daily Test

A 우리말 뜻과 일치하도록 빠진 글자를 써넣어 단어를 완성하세요.

1 열두 번째의　　　　t w e _ _ _ _ _

2 스무 번째의　　　　t w e n _ i _ _ _ _

3 열여섯 번째의　　　s i x _ _ _ e _ _ _

4 열한 번째의　　　　_ l _ v _ n _ _

5 열네 번째의　　　　f o u _ t _ _ n _ _

B 다음 영어 단어의 우리말 뜻을 쓰세요.

1 seventeenth ________________

2 thirteenth ________________

3 nineteenth ________________

4 fifteenth ________________

5 eighteenth ________________

C 우리말 뜻과 일치하도록 빈칸에 알맞은 단어를 써넣어 문장을 완성하세요.

1 The ________________ design is great.
열여섯 번째 디자인이 훌륭하다.

2 They sat in the ________________ row.
그들은 열일곱 번째 줄에 앉았다.

3 How much is the ________________ umbrella?
열세 번째 우산은 얼마인가요?

4 My ________________ birthday was a month ago.
나의 열두 번째 생일은 한 달 전이었다.

5 It's time to answer the ________________ question.
열한 번째 질문에 대답할 시간이다.

6 Is the ________________ player kicking a ball?
열아홉 번째 선수가 공을 차고 있니?

7 I received the ________________ call.
나는 열다섯 번째 전화를 받았다.

8 He hides the gift in the ________________ box.
그는 그 선물을 열네 번째 상자에 숨긴다.

01	**aisle** [ail]	몡 통로

I prefer an aisle seat.
나는 통로 쪽 좌석을 선호한다.

02	**basement** [béismənt]	몡 지하층, 지하실

I saw an old lamp in the basement.
나는 지하실에서 낡은 램프를 봤다.

03	**bridge** [bridʒ]	몡 다리

The bridge was closed because of an accident.
그 다리는 사고 때문에 폐쇄되었다.

04	**build** [bild]	통 짓다, 건설하다　✿ build-built-built

The city planned to build a new airport.
그 도시는 새 공항을 건설할 계획을 세웠다.

05	**building** [bíldiŋ]	몡 건물

The building is 50 meters high.
그 건물은 높이가 50미터이다.

06	**castle** [kǽsl]	몡 성

The king lived in the huge castle.
그 왕은 그 거대한 성에 살았다.

07	**ceiling** [síːliŋ]	몡 천장

A fan is hanging from the ceiling.
선풍기 한 대가 천장에 매달려 있다.

08	**elevator** [éləvèitər]	몡 엘리베이터

The elevator goes up to the fifth floor.
그 엘리베이터는 5층까지 올라간다.

09	**entrance** [éntrəns]	몡 입구, 문

The dogs are lying next to the entrance.
그 개들은 입구 옆에 누워 있다.

10	**fence** [fens]	몡 울타리

The horse jumped over the fence.
그 말은 울타리를 뛰어 넘었다.

Daily Test

A 우리말 뜻과 일치하도록 빠진 글자를 써넣어 단어를 완성하세요.

1 성 　　　_ _ s t _ _　　　2 입구, 문 　　　_ n _ _ a _ _ e

3 다리 　　　b _ _ _ g _　　　4 통로 　　　_ i _ _ e

5 건물 　　　_ u _ _ d _ _ g

B 다음 영어 단어의 우리말 뜻을 쓰세요.

1 elevator 　　　_______________　　　2 basement 　　　_______________

3 build 　　　_______________　　　4 ceiling 　　　_______________

5 fence 　　　_______________

C 우리말 뜻과 일치하도록 빈칸에 알맞은 단어를 써넣어 문장을 완성하세요.

1 The dogs are lying next to the _______________.
그 개들은 입구 옆에 누워 있다.

2 The king lived in the huge _______________.
그 왕은 그 거대한 성에 살았다.

3 I saw an old lamp in the _______________.
나는 지하실에서 낡은 램프를 봤다.

4 The _______________ goes up to the fifth floor.
그 엘리베이터는 5층까지 올라간다.

5 The horse jumped over the _______________.
그 말은 울타리를 뛰어 넘었다.

6 The _______________ is 50 meters high.
그 건물은 높이가 50미터이다.

7 The _______________ was closed because of an accident.
그 다리는 사고 때문에 폐쇄되었다.

8 A fan is hanging from the _______________.
선풍기 한 대가 천장에 매달려 있다.

11 garage
[gərá:ʤ]

🖲 명 차고, 주차장
Put the car in the garage!
그 차를 차고에 넣어!

12 hall
[hɔːl]

🖲 명 복도
Don't run in the hall.
복도에서 뛰지 마.

13 hut
[hʌt]

🖲 명 오두막
It was so hot, so we went to the hut.
너무 더워서, 우리는 오두막으로 갔다.

14 pyramid
[pírəmid]

🖲 명 피라미드
Visitors were surprised at the pyramid.
방문객들은 그 피라미드를 보고 놀랐다.

15 roof
[ru(:)f]

🖲 명 지붕
My brother must paint the roof.
나의 형은 그 지붕을 페인트칠해야 한다.

16 stairs
[stɛərz]

🖲 명 계단
My friends ran down the stairs.
나의 친구들은 계단을 뛰어 내려갔다.

17 structure
[strʌ́ktʃər]

🖲 명 구조, 구조물
This structure is made of wood.
이 구조물은 나무로 만들어졌다.

18 temple
[témpl]

🖲 명 절, 사원
We should be quiet in the temple.
우리는 사원 안에서 조용히 해야 한다.

19 tower
[táuər]

🖲 명 탑
The tower has a flag on the top.
그 탑은 꼭대기에 깃발이 있다.

20 wall
[wɔːl]

🖲 명 벽, 담
A thief was climbing the high wall.
도둑 한 명이 그 높은 담을 오르고 있었다.

Daily Test

A 우리말 뜻과 일치하도록 빠진 글자를 써넣어 단어를 완성하세요.

1 차고, 주차장   _ _ r _ g _

2 벽, 담   w _ _ _

3 탑   t _ _ e _

4 복도   _ _ l _

5 피라미드   _ _ r _ _ _ d

B 다음 영어 단어의 우리말 뜻을 쓰세요.

1 structure ________________

2 hut ________________

3 stairs ________________

4 roof ________________

5 temple ________________

C 우리말 뜻과 일치하도록 빈칸에 알맞은 단어를 써넣어 문장을 완성하세요.

1 Put the car in the ________________!
그 차를 차고에 넣어!

2 This ________________ is made of wood.
이 구조물은 나무로 만들어졌다.

3 It was so hot, so we went to the ________________.
너무 더워서, 우리는 오두막으로 갔다.

4 A thief was climbing the high ________________.
도둑 한 명이 그 높은 담을 오르고 있었다.

5 We should be quiet in the ________________.
우리는 사원 안에서 조용히 해야 한다.

6 My brother must paint the ________________.
나의 형은 그 지붕을 페인트칠해야 한다.

7 Visitors were surprised at the ________________.
방문객들은 그 피라미드를 보고 놀랐다.

8 The ________________ has a flag on the top.
그 탑은 꼭대기에 깃발이 있다.

Day 13 가정

01 adopt
[ədápt]

동 입양하다
The woman will adopt the twins.
그 여자는 그 쌍둥이를 입양할 것이다.

02 birth
[bəːrθ]

명 탄생, 출생 ✿ give birth to ~을 낳다
My aunt gave birth to a son.
나의 이모가 아들을 낳았다.

03 born
[bɔːrn]

형 태어난
She was born in 2000.
그녀는 2000년에 태어났다.

04 care
[kɛər]

명 돌봄, 보살핌 ✿ take care of ~을 돌보다
He takes care of those kids.
그는 저 아이들을 돌본다.

05 chore
[tʃɔːr]

명 (일상적인) 일
I finished house chores in thirty minutes.
나는 집안일을 30분 안에 끝냈다.

06 cook
[kuk]

동 요리하다
She always cooks chicken on Christmas.
그녀는 크리스마스에 항상 닭고기를 요리한다.

07 dishwashing
[díʃwɔ̀ːʃiŋ]

명 설거지
It is my turn for dishwashing.
내가 설거지를 할 차례이다.

08 feed
[fiːd]

동 먹이를 주다 ✿ feed-fed-fed
Mom told me to feed cows.
엄마는 소에게 먹이를 주라고 나에게 말씀하셨다.

09 fix
[fiks]

동 고치다
Grandpa will fix the broken chair.
할아버지가 그 부서진 의자를 고치실 것이다.

10 grow
[grou]

동 자라다 ✿ grow-grew-grown
Polly grew two centimeters in a month.
Polly는 한 달 동안 2센티미터 자랐다.

Daily Test

A 우리말 뜻과 일치하도록 빠진 글자를 써넣어 단어를 완성하세요.

1 자라다   __ r __ __ __   2 태어난   __ __ r __

3 요리하다   __ __ __ k   4 입양하다   __ d __ p __

5 탄생, 출생   b __ __ t __

B 다음 영어 단어의 우리말 뜻을 쓰세요.

1 care   __________________   2 fix   __________________

3 dishwashing   __________________   4 chore   __________________

5 feed   __________________

C 우리말 뜻과 일치하도록 빈칸에 알맞은 단어를 써넣어 문장을 완성하세요.

1 Polly ___________________ two centimeters in a month.
   Polly는 한 달 동안 2센티미터 자랐다.

2 The woman will ________________ the twins.
   그 여자는 그 쌍둥이를 입양할 것이다.

3 It is my turn for ________________ .
   내가 설거지를 할 차례이다.

4 She always ________________ chicken on Christmas.
   그녀는 크리스마스에 항상 닭고기를 요리한다.

5 Mom told me to ________________ cows.
   엄마는 소에게 먹이를 주라고 나에게 말씀하셨다.

6 Grandpa will ________________ the broken chair.
   할아버지가 그 부서진 의자를 고치실 것이다.

7 She was ________________ in 2000.
   그녀는 2000년에 태어났다.

8 I finished house ________________ in thirty minutes.
   나는 집안일을 30분 안에 끝냈다.

11 home
[houm]

(명) 집 ✿ at home 집에서
Let's have a Halloween party at home.
집에서 핼러윈 파티를 하자.

12 household
[háushòuld]

(명) 가정
Does the store sell household goods?
그 가게는 가정용품을 파니?

13 ironing
[áiərniŋ]

(명) 다리미질
The silk shirt needs ironing.
그 실크 셔츠는 다리미질이 필요하다.

14 laundry
[lɔ́ːndri]

(명) 세탁물, 세탁 ✿ do the laundry 세탁을 하다
I'm busy doing the laundry.
나는 세탁을 하느라 바쁘다.

15 lawn
[lɔːn]

(명) 잔디, 잔디밭
Did she forget to mow the lawn?
그녀는 잔디를 깎는 것을 잊었니?

16 love
[lʌv]

(명) 사랑 (동) 사랑하다
He loves all his family.
그는 그의 가족 모두를 사랑한다.

17 marriage
[mǽridʒ]

(명) 결혼 생활, 결혼
They have a happy marriage.
그들은 행복한 결혼 생활을 하고 있다.

18 marry
[mǽri]

(동) (~와) 결혼하다
She is going to marry the man.
그녀는 그 남자와 결혼할 것이다.

19 pregnant
[prégnənt]

(형) 임신한
My sister is pregnant with her first child.
나의 언니는 그녀의 첫 번째 아이를 임신 중이다.

20 raise
[reiz]

(동) 키우다
It is a good place to raise a kid.
그곳은 아이를 키우기에 좋은 곳이다.

Daily Test

A 우리말 뜻과 일치하도록 빠진 글자를 써넣어 단어를 완성하세요.

1 잔디, 잔디밭 l _ _ n
2 (~와) 결혼하다 _ a r _ _

3 임신한 _ _ e _ n _ _ t
4 키우다 _ _ i _ e

5 세탁물, 세탁 _ a _ n _ _ _

B 다음 영어 단어의 우리말 뜻을 쓰세요.

1 love _________________
2 home _________________

3 household _________________
4 marriage _________________

5 ironing _________________

C 우리말 뜻과 일치하도록 빈칸에 알맞은 단어를 써넣어 문장을 완성하세요.

1 She is going to _________________ the man.
그녀는 그 남자와 결혼할 것이다.

2 I'm busy doing the _________________.
나는 세탁을 하느라 바쁘다.

3 Does the store sell _________________ goods?
그 가게는 가정용품을 파니?

4 The silk shirt needs _________________.
그 실크 셔츠는 다리미질이 필요하다.

5 Did she forget to mow the _________________?
그녀는 잔디를 깎는 것을 잊었니?

6 It is a good place to _________________ a kid.
그곳은 아이를 키우기에 좋은 곳이다.

7 He _________________ all his family.
그는 그의 가족 모두를 사랑한다.

8 Let's have a Halloween party at _________________.
집에서 핼러윈 파티를 하자.

01 business
[bíznis]

명 사업, 업무
She succeeded in her business in China.
그녀는 중국에서 사업에 성공했다.

02 change
[tʃeindʒ]

동 변하다, 바꾸다   명 변화
He changed the training program.
그는 그 훈련 프로그램을 바꿨다.

03 community
[kəmjúːnəti]

명 지역 사회, 지역 주민
She teaches knitting at the community center.
그녀는 지역 주민 회관에서 뜨개질을 가르친다.

04 crowd
[kraud]

명 사람들, 군중, 무리
He gave a speech to the crowd.
그는 군중에게 연설을 했다.

05 donate
[dóuneit]

동 기부하다
Students can also donate in various ways.
학생들도 여러 가지 방법으로 기부할 수 있다.

06 gather
[gǽðər]

동 모이다, 모으다
The bus users gathered together.
그 버스 이용자들은 함께 모였다.

07 group
[gruːp]

명 그룹, 집단
He divided them into three groups.
그는 그들을 세 개의 그룹으로 나누었다.

08 lack
[læk]

명 부족, 결핍
A lack of water is a global problem.
물 부족은 전 세계적인 문제이다.

09 learn
[ləːrn]

동 배우다
It is important to learn history.
역사를 배우는 것은 중요하다.

10 main
[mein]

형 주된
Recycling is our main project.
재활용은 우리의 주요 프로젝트이다.

Daily Test

A 우리말 뜻과 일치하도록 빠진 글자를 써넣어 단어를 완성하세요.

1 기부하다   __ __ n a __ __

2 그룹, 집단   __ __ __ u p

3 주된   m __ __ __

4 모이다, 모으다   __ a __ __ e __

5 배우다   __ __ a r __

B 다음 영어 단어의 우리말 뜻을 쓰세요.

1 business   _______________

2 crowd   _______________

3 lack   _______________

4 community   _______________

5 change   _______________

C 우리말 뜻과 일치하도록 빈칸에 알맞은 단어를 써넣어 문장을 완성하세요.

1 Students can also _______________ in various ways.
학생들도 여러 가지 방법으로 기부할 수 있다.

2 Recycling is our _______________ project.
재활용은 우리의 주요 프로젝트이다.

3 He gave a speech to the _______________.
그는 군중에게 연설을 했다.

4 A _______________ of water is a global problem.
물 부족은 전 세계적인 문제이다.

5 He _______________ the training program.
그는 그 훈련 프로그램을 바꿨다.

6 He divided them into three _______________.
그는 그들을 세 개의 그룹으로 나누었다.

7 She succeeded in her _______________ in China.
그녀는 중국에서 사업에 성공했다.

8 The bus users _______________ together.
그 버스 이용자들은 함께 모였다.

11 member
[mémbər]

명 구성원, 회원
The team members are proud of their job.
그 팀 구성원들은 그들의 일을 자랑스러워한다.

12 pass
[pæs]

동 합격하다
Did he pass the exam?
그는 그 시험에 합격했니?

13 presentation
[prìːzəntéiʃən]

명 발표
What is the topic of their presentation?
그들의 발표 주제는 무엇이니?

14 print
[print]

동 인쇄하다
She didn't print her report.
그녀는 그녀의 보고서를 인쇄하지 않았다.

15 promise
[prámis]

동 약속하다
They promised to call me.
그들은 나에게 전화하겠다고 약속했다.

16 question
[kwéstʃən]

명 질문, 문제
Do you have any questions?
질문 있나요?

17 role
[roul]

명 역할
What is your role in the meeting?
그 모임에서 너의 역할은 무엇이니?

18 speak
[spiːk]

동 말하다 ✿ speak-spoke-spoken
I need to speak to Cindy about this.
나는 이것에 대해서 Cindy와 이야기해야 한다.

19 think
[θiŋk]

동 생각하다 ✿ think-thought-thought
The man was thinking very carefully.
그 남자는 매우 신중하게 생각하고 있었다.

20 write
[rait]

동 쓰다 ✿ write-wrote-written
The writer started to write a story.
그 작가는 이야기 한 편을 쓰기 시작했다.

Daily Test

A 우리말 뜻과 일치하도록 빠진 글자를 써넣어 단어를 완성하세요.

1 합격하다   __ a __ __

2 말하다   s __ __ __ k

3 역할   __ __ l __

4 생각하다   __ h __ n __

5 인쇄하다   __ __ i __ t

B 다음 영어 단어의 우리말 뜻을 쓰세요.

1 write   ___________________

2 member   ___________________

3 promise   ___________________

4 question   ___________________

5 presentation   ___________________

C 우리말 뜻과 일치하도록 빈칸에 알맞은 단어를 써넣어 문장을 완성하세요.

1 What is your ___________________ in the meeting?
그 모임에서 너의 역할은 무엇이니?

2 They ___________________ to call me.
그들은 나에게 전화하겠다고 약속했다.

3 The team ___________________ are proud of their job.
그 팀 구성원들은 그들의 일을 자랑스러워한다.

4 Did he ___________________ the exam?
그는 그 시험에 합격했니?

5 What is the topic of their ___________________?
그들의 발표 주제는 무엇이니?

6 The writer started to ___________________ a story.
그 작가는 이야기 한 편을 쓰기 시작했다.

7 The man was ___________________ very carefully.
그 남자는 매우 신중하게 생각하고 있었다.

8 She didn't ___________________ her report.
그녀는 그녀의 보고서를 인쇄하지 않았다.

A 우리말 뜻에 해당하는 영어 단어를 찾아 동그라미 하세요.

| 사랑; 사랑하다 | 열두 번째의 | 지붕 | 요리하다 | 사람들, 군중 |
| 태어난 | 여섯 번째의 | 성 | 부족, 결핍 | 인쇄하다 |

c	r	c	z	s	t	l	a	c	k
y	b	o	r	n	b	n	o	z	t
c	b	o	b	p	x	r	k	v	w
a	v	k	g	v	x	c	f	c	e
s	i	x	t	h	h	o	d	v	l
t	j	s	k	f	o	h	r	k	f
l	f	g	p	r	i	n	t	g	t
e	q	c	r	o	w	d	k	h	h

B 우리말 뜻과 일치하도록 알맞은 단어를 골라 문장을 완성하세요.

| eighteenth | care | community | build | stairs | tenth |

1 My friends ran down the ________________.
나의 친구들은 계단을 뛰어 내려갔다.

2 She teaches knitting at the ________________ center.
그녀는 지역 주민 회관에서 뜨개질을 가르친다.

3 The ________________ boy raised his hand.
열여덟 번째 소년이 손을 들었다.

4 The city planned to ________________ a new airport.
그 도시는 새 공항을 건설할 계획을 세웠다.

5 He takes ________________ of those kids.
그는 저 아이들을 돌본다.

6 The runner took ________________ place.
그 주자는 10등을 차지했다.

Day 15

Day 15_C

C 들려 주는 영어 단어를 바르게 쓴 다음, 우리말 뜻을 써넣으세요.

	영어 단어	우리말		영어 단어	우리말
1			11		
2			12		
3			13		
4			14		
5			15		
6			16		
7			17		
8			18		
9			19		
10			20		

D 우리말 뜻과 일치하도록 알맞은 단어를 골라 동그라미 하세요.

1 My aunt gave (chore / birth) to a son.
나의 이모가 아들을 낳았다.

2 Don't run in the (wall / hall).
복도에서 뛰지 마.

3 It is important to (donate / learn) history.
역사를 배우는 것은 중요하다.

4 Do you have any (questions / members)?
질문 있나요?

5 We were working on the (thirteenth / twentieth) floor.
우리는 20층에서 일을 하고 있었다.

6 They have a happy (marriage / laundry).
그들은 행복한 결혼 생활을 하고 있다.

E 영어는 우리말로, 우리말은 영어로 바꿔 쓰세요.

1	fourth	_____________	2 열아홉 번째의	_____________
3	promise	_____________	4 오두막	_____________
5	temple	_____________	6 엘리베이터	_____________
7	marry	_____________	8 생각하다	_____________
9	home	_____________	10 일곱 번째의	_____________
11	bridge	_____________	12 구성원, 회원	_____________
13	change	_____________	14 세탁물, 세탁	_____________
15	thirteenth	_____________	16 고치다	_____________
17	gather	_____________	18 입양하다	_____________
19	entrance	_____________	20 열다섯 번째의	_____________

Day 15_F

F 잘 듣고, 빈칸에 알맞은 단어를 써넣어 문장을 완성하세요.

1 Mom told me to _____________ cows.

2 Today is your _____________ day at school.

3 A fan is hanging from the _____________.

4 He divided them into three _____________.

5 The _____________ has a flag on the top.

6 The _____________ design is great.

7 Did he _____________ the exam?

8 Did she forget to mow the _____________?

G 우리말 뜻과 일치하도록 빈칸에 알맞은 단어를 써넣어 문장을 완성하세요.

1 I need to s_______________ to Cindy about this.
나는 이것에 대해서 Cindy와 이야기해야 한다.

2 I prefer an a_______________ seat.
나는 통로 쪽 좌석을 선호한다.

3 It is my turn for d_______________.
내가 설거지를 할 차례이다.

4 Please read the n_______________ sentence.
아홉 번째 문장을 읽어 주세요.

5 It's time to answer the e_______________ question.
열한 번째 질문에 대답할 시간이다.

6 My sister is p_______________ with her first child.
나의 언니는 그녀의 첫 번째 아이를 임신 중이다.

7 She succeeded in her b_______________ in China.
그녀는 중국에서 사업에 성공했다.

8 Does the store sell h_______________ goods?
그 가게는 가정용품을 파니?

9 T_______________ grade students learn English.
3학년 학생들은 영어를 배운다.

10 This s_______________ is made of wood.
이 구조물은 나무로 만들어졌다.

✎ Review에서 틀린 문제의 영어 단어와 우리말 뜻을 쓴 다음, 영어 단어를 3번씩 쓰세요.

	( )	_______ _______ _______
	( )	_______ _______ _______
	( )	_______ _______ _______
	( )	_______ _______ _______
	( )	_______ _______ _______

01 bean
[biːn]

명 콩
First, you need to wash these beans.
먼저, 너희는 이 콩을 씻어야 한다.

02 broccoli
[brákəli]

명 브로콜리
Where can I buy broccoli?
브로콜리를 어디에서 살 수 있니?

03 crab
[kræb]

명 게
The bird can't eat the crabs.
그 새는 그 게들을 먹을 수 없다.

04 cucumber
[kjúːkʌmbər]

명 오이
The sandwich has cucumbers in it.
그 샌드위치는 안에 오이가 들어 있다.

05 ginger
[dʒíndʒər]

명 생강
Ginger is a kind of root vegetable.
생강은 뿌리채소의 한 종류이다.

06 kiwi
[kíːwi(ː)]

명 키위
A kiwi is rich in vitamin C.
키위는 비타민 C가 풍부하다.

07 lettuce
[létis]

명 상추
What fresh lettuce it is!
그것은 매우 신선한 상추이구나!

08 melon
[mélən]

명 멜론
The men carried ten melons.
그 남자들은 멜론 열 개를 날랐다.

09 nut
[nʌt]

명 견과
My family eats nuts once a day.
나의 가족은 하루에 한 번 견과류를 먹는다.

10 plum
[plʌm]

명 자두
Dried plums are often used for cooking.
말린 자두는 요리에 자주 사용된다.

A 우리말 뜻과 일치하도록 빠진 글자를 써넣어 단어를 완성하세요.

1 콩   __ e __ n   **2** 게   c __ __ __

3 멜론   __ __ __ o n   **4** 키위   __ __ w __

5 오이   __ __ c __ m __ __ r

B 다음 영어 단어의 우리말 뜻을 쓰세요.

1 plum   _________________   **2** nut   _________________

3 ginger   _________________   **4** broccoli   _________________

5 lettuce   _________________

C 우리말 뜻과 일치하도록 빈칸에 알맞은 단어를 써넣어 문장을 완성하세요.

1 Dried _________________ are often used for cooking.
말린 자두는 요리에 자주 사용된다.

2 A _________________ is rich in vitamin C.
키위는 비타민 C가 풍부하다.

3 First, you need to wash these _________________.
먼저, 너희는 이 콩을 씻어야 한다.

4 The men carried ten _________________.
그 남자들은 멜론 열 개를 날랐다.

5 Where can I buy _________________?
브로콜리를 어디에서 살 수 있니?

6 What fresh _________________ it is!
그것은 매우 신선한 상추이구나!

7 _________________ is a kind of root vegetable.
생강은 뿌리채소의 한 종류이다.

8 The bird can't eat the _________________.
그 새는 그 게들을 먹을 수 없다.

11	**pumpkin** [pʌ́mpkin]	명 호박 Let's make cookies with pumpkins. 호박으로 쿠키를 만들자.
12	**seafood** [síːfùːd]	명 해산물 That's why she loves seafood. 그것이 그녀가 해산물을 정말 좋아하는 이유이다.
13	**shellfish** [ʃélfiʃ]	명 조개류 I have an allergy to shellfish. 나는 조개류에 알레르기가 있다.
14	**shrimp** [ʃrimp]	명 새우 There are not any shrimps in the pot. 냄비 안에 새우가 하나도 없다.
15	**spinach** [spínitʃ]	명 시금치 Did she grind spinach with apples? 그녀는 시금치를 사과와 함께 갈았니?
16	**squid** [skwid]	명 오징어 Squids got caught in the net. 오징어들이 그물에 걸렸다.
17	**strawberry** [strɔ́ːbèri]	명 딸기 Strawberry seeds are tiny. 딸기 씨들은 아주 작다.
18	**sweet potato** [swìːtpətéitou]	명 고구마 He put the sweet potatoes in the oven. 그는 오븐에 그 고구마들을 넣었다.
19	**tomato** [təméitou]	명 토마토 When is she going to pick the tomatoes? 그녀는 언제 그 토마토들을 딸 거니?
20	**watermelon** [wɔ́ːtərmèlən]	명 수박 Ann cut a watermelon into several pieces. Ann은 수박을 여러 조각으로 잘랐다.

Daily Test

A 우리말 뜻과 일치하도록 빠진 글자를 써넣어 단어를 완성하세요.

1 오징어   s __ __ i __

2 토마토   __ o __ __ t __

3 해산물   __ __ a f __ __ __ __

4 새우   __ h __ __ m __

5 딸기   __ __ r __ w __ __ __ __ y

B 다음 영어 단어의 우리말 뜻을 쓰세요.

1 spinach   _________________

2 shellfish   _________________

3 pumpkin   _________________

4 watermelon   _________________

5 sweet potato   _________________

C 우리말 뜻과 일치하도록 빈칸에 알맞은 단어를 써넣어 문장을 완성하세요.

1 There are not any _________________ in the pot.
냄비 안에 새우가 하나도 없다.

2 _________________ seeds are tiny.
딸기 씨들은 아주 작다.

3 When is she going to pick the _________________?
그녀는 언제 그 토마토들을 딸 거니?

4 _________________ got caught in the net.
오징어들이 그물에 걸렸다.

5 I have an allergy to _________________.
나는 조개류에 알레르기가 있다.

6 He put the _________________ in the oven.
그는 오븐에 그 고구마들을 넣었다.

7 Ann cut a _________________ into several pieces.
Ann은 수박을 여러 조각으로 잘랐다.

8 Did she grind _________________ with apples?
그녀는 시금치를 사과와 함께 갈았니?

 **Day 17** 건강과 질병

01 cancer
[kǽnsər]

명 암
The doctor found cancer in his body.
그 의사는 그의 몸에서 암을 발견했다.

02 cold
[kould]

명 감기　✿ catch a cold 감기에 걸리다
I caught a cold, so I have a runny nose.
나는 감기에 걸려서, 콧물이 난다.

03 cough
[kɔ(:)f]

동 기침하다　명 기침
She is at home with a bad cough.
그녀는 심한 기침 때문에 집에 있다.

04 death
[deθ]

명 죽음
The firefighters are not afraid of death.
그 소방관들은 죽음을 무서워하지 않는다.

05 die
[dai]

동 죽다
He died at the age of 40.
그는 40세에 죽었다.

06 diet
[dáiət]

명 식단, 다이어트　✿ go on a diet 다이어트를 하다
He doesn't have to go on a diet.
그는 다이어트를 할 필요가 없다.

07 disease
[dizíːz]

명 질병
This disease can be cured completely.
이 질병은 완전히 치료될 수 있다.

08 dizzy
[dízi]

형 어지러운
My brother felt dizzy after rolling.
나의 남동생은 구르기를 한 후에 어지러움을 느꼈다.

09 fever
[fíːvər]

명 열
The girl's fever didn't go down.
그 소녀의 열이 내려가지 않았다.

10 headache
[hédèik]

명 두통
She couldn't sleep because of a headache.
그녀는 두통 때문에 잠을 잘 수 없었다.

Daily Test

A 우리말 뜻과 일치하도록 빠진 글자를 써넣어 단어를 완성하세요.

1 열   f __ v __ __ __

2 암   __ a __ __ e __

3 죽다   __ __ e

4 어지러운   __ __ z __ y

5 기침하다; 기침   __ __ u __ h

B 다음 영어 단어의 우리말 뜻을 쓰세요.

1 disease   __________________

2 cold   __________________

3 headache   __________________

4 diet   __________________

5 death   __________________

C 우리말 뜻과 일치하도록 빈칸에 알맞은 단어를 써넣어 문장을 완성하세요.

1 She couldn't sleep because of a __________________.
그녀는 두통 때문에 잠을 잘 수 없었다.

2 The firefighters are not afraid of __________________.
그 소방관들은 죽음을 무서워하지 않는다.

3 The doctor found __________________ in his body.
그 의사는 그의 몸에서 암을 발견했다.

4 She is at home with a bad __________________.
그녀는 심한 기침 때문에 집에 있다.

5 This __________________ can be cured completely.
이 질병은 완전히 치료될 수 있다.

6 I caught a __________________, so I have a runny nose.
나는 감기에 걸려서, 콧물이 난다.

7 The girl's __________________ didn't go down.
그 소녀의 열이 내려가지 않았다.

8 He __________________ at the age of 40.
그는 40세에 죽었다.

Day 17   건강과 질병

11 heal
[hiːl]

동 치유하다, 치유되다
It will take three weeks to heal the cut.
그 상처를 치유하는 데에 3주가 걸릴 것이다.

12 health
[helθ]

명 건강   ✿ keep one's health 건강을 지키다
What do you do to keep your health?
너는 너의 건강을 지키기 위해 무엇을 하니?

13 hurt
[həːrt]

동 다치게 하다, 아프다   ✿ hurt-hurt-hurt
Ouch! My toes hurt.
아야! 내 발가락이 아파.

14 medicine
[médisin]

명 약
Did you take the medicine?
너는 그 약을 먹었니?

15 pale
[peil]

형 창백한, 핼쑥한
Tom looked pale this morning.
Tom은 오늘 아침에 창백해 보였다.

16 patient
[péiʃənt]

명 환자
The patient wanted to express thanks.
그 환자는 감사를 표하고 싶어 했다.

17 pill
[pil]

명 알약, 정제
I take this vitamin pill every day.
나는 이 비타민제를 매일 먹는다.

18 sick
[sik]

형 아픈, 병든
He was sick, but he didn't leave early.
그는 아팠지만, 일찍 떠나지 않았다.

19 sneeze
[sniːz]

동 재채기하다
Did she sneeze in the library?
그녀는 도서관에서 재채기했니?

20 stomachache
[stʌ́məkèik]

명 위통, 복통
Cold food can cause a stomachache.
찬 음식은 복통을 일으킬 수 있다.

Ⓐ 우리말 뜻과 일치하도록 빠진 글자를 써넣어 단어를 완성하세요.

1 환자   __ __ t __ e __ __

2 다치게 하다, 아프다   __ u __ __

3 아픈, 병든   __ __ __ k

4 치유하다, 치유되다   __ __ a __

5 약   __ e d __ __ __ __ __

Ⓑ 다음 영어 단어의 우리말 뜻을 쓰세요.

1 stomachache   __________________

2 health   __________________

3 pale   __________________

4 sneeze   __________________

5 pill   __________________

Ⓒ 우리말 뜻과 일치하도록 빈칸에 알맞은 단어를 써넣어 문장을 완성하세요.

1 It will take three weeks to __________________ the cut.
그 상처를 치유하는 데에 3주가 걸릴 것이다.

2 He was __________________, but he didn't leave early.
그는 아팠지만, 일찍 떠나지 않았다.

3 Tom looked __________________ this morning.
Tom은 오늘 아침에 창백해 보였다.

4 Cold food can cause a __________________.
찬 음식은 복통을 일으킬 수 있다.

5 Ouch! My toes __________________.
아야! 내 발가락이 아파.

6 Did she __________________ in the library?
그녀는 도서관에서 재채기했니?

7 The __________________ wanted to express thanks.
그 환자는 감사를 표하고 싶어 했다.

8 What do you do to keep your __________________?
너는 너의 건강을 지키기 위해 무엇을 하니?

01	**agree** [əgríː]	동 동의하다 She didn't agree with me. 그녀는 나에게 동의하지 않았다.
02	**announce** [ənáuns]	동 발표하다, 알리다 They are going to announce the result. 그들은 그 결과를 발표할 것이다.
03	**answer** [ǽnsər]	명 대답 동 대답하다 My brother didn't hear my answer. 나의 오빠는 나의 대답을 듣지 못했다.
04	**ask** [æsk]	동 묻다, 물어보다 Ask him, and he'll answer kindly. 그에게 물어봐, 그러면 그가 친절하게 대답할 거야.
05	**call** [kɔːl]	동 전화하다 명 전화 He missed a call from his mom. 그는 그의 엄마에게서 온 전화를 놓쳤다.
06	**chat** [tʃæt]	동 담소를 나누다 명 담소 I had a short chat with Susie. 나는 Susie와 짧은 담소를 나누었다.
07	**communicate** [kəmjúːnəkèit]	동 의사소통을 하다 We can communicate by paintings, too. 우리는 그림으로도 의사소통을 할 수 있다.
08	**computer** [kəmpjúːtər]	명 컴퓨터 Computers are changing our lives. 컴퓨터는 우리의 삶을 바꾸고 있다.
09	**disagree** [dìsəgríː]	동 동의하지 않다 I disagree with their idea this time. 나는 이번에는 그들의 생각에 동의하지 않는다.
10	**explain** [ikspléin]	동 설명하다 He explained how to grow corn. 그는 옥수수를 기르는 방법을 설명했다.

Daily Test

A 우리말 뜻과 일치하도록 빠진 글자를 써넣어 단어를 완성하세요.

1 대답; 대답하다   __ n s __ __ __ __

2 컴퓨터   __ __ m __ __ t __ r

3 전화하다; 전화   __ a __ __

4 동의하다   __ __ r __ __

5 발표하다, 알리다   a __ __ o __ __ c __

B 다음 영어 단어의 우리말 뜻을 쓰세요.

1 chat _________________

2 communicate _________________

3 disagree _________________

4 ask _________________

5 explain _________________

C 우리말 뜻과 일치하도록 빈칸에 알맞은 단어를 써넣어 문장을 완성하세요.

1 He _________________ how to grow corn.
그는 옥수수를 기르는 방법을 설명했다.

2 My brother didn't hear my _________________.
나의 오빠는 나의 대답을 듣지 못했다.

3 _________________ are changing our lives.
컴퓨터는 우리의 삶을 바꾸고 있다.

4 They are going to _________________ the result.
그들은 그 결과를 발표할 것이다.

5 I _________________ with their idea this time.
나는 이번에는 그들의 생각에 동의하지 않는다.

6 _________________ him, and he'll answer kindly.
그에게 물어봐, 그러면 그가 친절하게 대답할 거야.

7 We can _________________ by paintings, too.
우리는 그림으로도 의사소통을 할 수 있다.

8 He missed a _________________ from his mom.
그는 그의 엄마에게서 온 전화를 놓쳤다.

11 fact
[fækt]

명 사실
The book is full of interesting facts about animals.
그 책은 동물에 대한 흥미로운 사실들로 가득하다.

12 gesture
[dʒéstʃər]

명 몸짓, 제스처
What does his gesture mean?
그의 몸짓은 무엇을 의미하니?

13 humor
[hjúːmər]

명 유머, 익살   ✿ a sense of humor 유머 감각
The singer has a good sense of humor.
그 가수는 유머 감각이 좋다.

14 inform
[infɔ́ːrm]

동 (공식적으로) 알리다
Inform the police right now.
당장 경찰에 알려.

15 Internet
[íntəːrnet]

명 인터넷
Will they collect data through the Internet?
그들은 인터넷으로 자료를 모을 거니?

16 joke
[dʒouk]

명 농담
She smiled at my joke.
그녀는 나의 농담에 미소를 지었다.

17 letter
[létər]

명 편지
Where did the letter come from?
그 편지는 어디에서 왔니?

18 mail
[meil]

명 우편, 우편물
We had a lot of mail today.
우리는 오늘 많은 우편물을 받았다.

19 news
[njuːz]

명 소식, 뉴스
We are happy to hear the news.
우리는 그 소식을 듣게 되어 행복하다.

20 phone
[foun]

명 전화기
Kathy bought a new phone.
Kathy는 새 전화기를 샀다.

Daily Test

A 우리말 뜻과 일치하도록 빠진 글자를 써넣어 단어를 완성하세요.

1 편지　　　　　__ e __ __ e __　　　　2 사실　　　　　__ __ __ t

3 유머, 익살　　__ __ m __ r　　　　　4 소식, 뉴스　　__ __ __ s

5 인터넷　　　　__ __ t __ __ n __ t

B 다음 영어 단어의 우리말 뜻을 쓰세요.

1 mail　　＿＿＿＿＿＿＿＿　　2 joke　　＿＿＿＿＿＿＿＿

3 gesture　＿＿＿＿＿＿＿＿　　4 inform　＿＿＿＿＿＿＿＿

5 phone　　＿＿＿＿＿＿＿＿

C 우리말 뜻과 일치하도록 빈칸에 알맞은 단어를 써넣어 문장을 완성하세요.

1 Will they collect data through the ＿＿＿＿＿＿＿＿?
　그들은 인터넷으로 자료를 모을 거니?

2 What does his ＿＿＿＿＿＿＿＿ mean?
　그의 몸짓은 무엇을 의미하니?

3 Kathy bought a new ＿＿＿＿＿＿＿＿.
　Kathy는 새 전화기를 샀다.

4 We are happy to hear the ＿＿＿＿＿＿＿＿.
　우리는 그 소식을 듣게 되어 행복하다.

5 Where did the ＿＿＿＿＿＿＿＿ come from?
　그 편지는 어디에서 왔니?

6 The book is full of interesting ＿＿＿＿＿＿＿＿ about animals.
　그 책은 동물에 대한 흥미로운 사실들로 가득하다.

7 She smiled at my ＿＿＿＿＿＿＿＿.
　그녀는 나의 농담에 미소를 지었다.

8 We had a lot of ＿＿＿＿＿＿＿＿ today.
　우리는 오늘 많은 우편물을 받았다.

 **Day 19** 때와 시기

01 after
[ǽftər]

전 접 ~ 뒤에, ~ 후에
The train will leave after an hour.
그 기차는 한 시간 후에 출발할 것이다.

02 afternoon
[æ̀ːftərnúːn]

명 오후
He stayed at home in the afternoon.
그는 오후에 집에 머물렀다.

03 ago
[əgóu]

부 (얼마의 시간) 전에
We moved here five months ago.
우리는 다섯 달 전에 여기로 이사했다.

04 before
[bifɔ́ːr]

전 접 ~ 전에, ~ 앞에
Let's warm up before we run.
달리기 전에 준비 운동을 하자.

05 dawn
[dɔːn]

명 새벽
She went to bed at dawn.
그녀는 새벽에 잠자리에 들었다.

06 during
[djú(ː)əriŋ]

전 ~ 동안, ~ 내내
What will he do during the vacation?
그는 방학 동안 무엇을 할 거니?

07 early
[ɔ́ːrli]

형 이른 부 일찍
She arrived at school early.
그녀는 학교에 일찍 도착했다.

08 end
[end]

명 끝, 종료
We have a party at the end of the year.
우리는 연말에 파티가 있다.

09 evening
[íːvniŋ]

명 저녁
I usually take a bath in the evening.
나는 보통 저녁에 목욕을 한다.

10 forever
[fərévər]

부 영원히
Tim will remember them forever.
Tim은 그들을 영원히 기억할 것이다.

Daily Test

A 우리말 뜻과 일치하도록 빠진 글자를 써넣어 단어를 완성하세요.

1 ~ 전에, ~ 앞에   b __ __ o __ __

2 영원히   __ __ r __ v __ __

3 이른; 일찍   __ a __ __ y

4 새벽   __ __ w __

5 오후   __ __ t __ __ n o __ __

B 다음 영어 단어의 우리말 뜻을 쓰세요.

1 evening   _______________

2 ago   _______________

3 end   _______________

4 during   _______________

5 after   _______________

C 우리말 뜻과 일치하도록 빈칸에 알맞은 단어를 써넣어 문장을 완성하세요.

1 What will he do _______________ the vacation?
그는 방학 동안 무엇을 할 거니?

2 The train will leave _______________ an hour.
그 기차는 한 시간 후에 출발할 것이다.

3 Let's warm up _______________ we run.
달리기 전에 준비 운동을 하자.

4 He stayed at home in the _______________.
그는 오후에 집에 머물렀다.

5 She arrived at school _______________.
그녀는 학교에 일찍 도착했다.

6 I usually take a bath in the _______________.
나는 보통 저녁에 목욕을 한다.

7 We moved here five months _______________.
우리는 다섯 달 전에 여기로 이사했다.

8 Tim will remember them _______________.
Tim은 그들을 영원히 기억할 것이다.

11　future
[fjú:tʃər]

명 미래　형 미래의
Can you imagine your future?
너는 너의 미래를 상상할 수 있니?

12　last
[læst]

한 지난, 마지막의
They visited England last winter.
그들은 지난겨울에 영국을 방문했다.

13　late
[leit]

형 늦은　부 늦게
I'm sorry I'm late.
늦어서 미안해.

14　midnight
[mídnàit]

명 자정, 밤 12시
The store is open from 10 a.m. to midnight.
그 가게는 오전 10시부터 밤 12시까지 연다.

15　morning
[mɔ́:rniŋ]

명 아침
Jake goes to the gym every morning.
Jake는 매일 아침 체육관에 간다.

16　next
[nekst]

형 다음의　부 그 다음에
I will watch this movie next time.
나는 이 영화를 다음 번에 볼 것이다.

17　night
[nait]

명 밤
Would you turn off the music at night?
밤에는 음악을 꺼 줄래?

18　noon
[nu:n]

명 정오, 낮 12시
The meeting will start at noon.
그 회의는 낮 12시에 시작할 것이다.

19　past
[pæst]

명 과거　형 지난, 이전의
Some men wore skirts in the past.
과거에 어떤 남자들은 치마를 입었다.

20　present
[prézənt]

명 현재　형 현재의
The tradition continues to the present.
그 전통은 현재까지 계속된다.

Daily Test

A 우리말 뜻과 일치하도록 빠진 글자를 써넣어 단어를 완성하세요.

1 아침   m __ __ __ __ n __   **2** 정오, 낮 12시   __ __ __ n

3 밤   __ i __ __ t   **4** 다음의; 그 다음에   __ e __ __

5 현재; 현재의   __ r __ s __ __ __

B 다음 영어 단어의 우리말 뜻을 쓰세요.

1 midnight   ________________   **2** past   ________________

3 future   ________________   **4** last   ________________

5 late   ________________

C 우리말 뜻과 일치하도록 빈칸에 알맞은 단어를 써넣어 문장을 완성하세요.

1 The store is open from 10 a.m. to ________________.
그 가게는 오전 10시부터 밤 12시까지 연다.

2 Can you imagine your ________________?
너는 너의 미래를 상상할 수 있니?

3 Some men wore skirts in the ________________.
과거에 어떤 남자들은 치마를 입었다.

4 They visited England ________________ winter.
그들은 지난겨울에 영국을 방문했다.

5 The meeting will start at ________________.
그 회의는 낮 12시에 시작할 것이다.

6 Jake goes to the gym every ________________.
Jake는 매일 아침 체육관에 간다.

7 Would you turn off the music at ________________?
밤에는 음악을 꺼 줄래?

8 The tradition continues to the ________________.
그 전통은 현재까지 계속된다.

A 우리말 뜻에 해당하는 영어 단어를 찾아 동그라미 하세요.

| 지난, 마지막의 | 키워 | 전화하다; 전화 | 게 | 우편, 우편물 |
| 오징어 | 정오, 낮 12시 | 이른; 일찍 | 감기 | 치유하다, 치유되다 |

m	z	k	i	w	i	j	n	y	h
a	c	q	s	d	t	p	g	h	p
i	r	t	b	s	y	c	h	e	r
l	a	s	a	d	k	t	a	a	c
c	b	l	x	n	o	o	n	l	o
e	a	r	l	y	h	j	k	j	l
x	t	m	g	x	s	y	w	l	d
j	s	q	u	i	d	p	z	h	n

B 우리말 뜻과 일치하도록 알맞은 단어를 골라 문장을 완성하세요.

| dizzy | pumpkins | pill | chat | next | humor |

1 I will watch this movie _______________ time.
나는 이 영화를 다음 번에 볼 것이다.

2 Let's make cookies with _______________.
호박으로 쿠키를 만들자.

3 The singer has a good sense of _______________.
그 가수는 유머 감각이 좋다.

4 I take this vitamin _______________ every day.
나는 이 비타민제를 매일 먹는다.

5 I had a short _______________ with Susie.
나는 Susie와 짧은 담소를 나누었다.

6 My brother felt _______________ after rolling.
나의 남동생은 구르기를 한 후에 어지러움을 느꼈다.

Day 20

Day 20_C

C 들려 주는 영어 단어를 바르게 쓴 다음, 우리말 뜻을 써넣으세요.

	영어 단어	우리말		영어 단어	우리말
1			11		
2			12		
3			13		
4			14		
5			15		
6			16		
7			17		
8			18		
9			19		
10			20		

D 우리말 뜻과 일치하도록 알맞은 단어를 골라 동그라미 하세요.

1 I'm sorry I'm (past / late).
   늦어서 미안해.

2 She didn't (agree / answer) with me.
   그녀는 나에게 동의하지 않았다.

3 The doctor found (cancer / cough) in his body.
   그 의사는 그의 몸에서 암을 발견했다.

4 That's why she loves (spinach / seafood).
   그것이 그녀가 해산물을 정말 좋아하는 이유이다.

5 The train will leave (before / after) an hour.
   그 기차는 한 시간 후에 출발할 것이다.

6 The sandwich has (cucumbers / beans) in it.
   그 샌드위치는 안에 오이가 들어 있다.

1	ask	___________	2	새벽	___________
3	die	___________	4	브로콜리	___________
5	gesture	___________	6	과거; 지난	___________
7	hurt	___________	8	두통	___________
9	ago	___________	10	멜론	___________
11	forever	___________	12	동의하지 않다	___________
13	phone	___________	14	수박	___________
15	midnight	___________	16	시금치	___________
17	sick	___________	18	위통, 복통	___________
19	sweet potato	___________	20	편지	___________

Day 20_F

F 잘 듣고, 빈칸에 알맞은 단어를 써넣어 문장을 완성하세요.

1 We have a party at the _______________ of the year.

2 The tradition continues to the _______________.

3 Did you take the _______________?

4 He doesn't have to go on a _______________.

5 There are not any _______________ in the pot.

6 My family eats _______________ once a day.

7 _______________ the police right now.

8 _______________ are changing our lives.

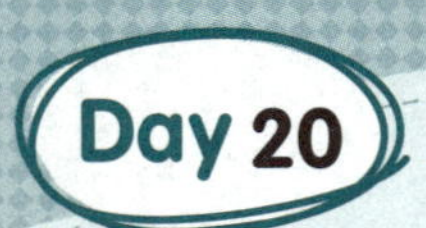

G 우리말 뜻과 일치하도록 빈칸에 알맞은 단어를 써넣어 문장을 완성하세요.

1 They are going to a_________________ the result.
그들은 그 결과를 발표할 것이다.

2 Jake goes to the gym every m_________________.
Jake는 매일 아침 체육관에 간다.

3 G_________________ is a kind of root vegetable.
생강은 뿌리채소의 한 종류이다.

4 Tom looked p_________________ this morning.
Tom은 오늘 아침에 창백해 보였다.

5 Will they collect data through the I_________________?
그들은 인터넷으로 자료를 모을 거니?

6 I have an allergy to s_________________.
나는 조개류에 알레르기가 있다.

7 I usually take a bath in the e_________________.
나는 보통 저녁에 목욕을 한다.

8 The firefighters are not afraid of d_________________.
그 소방관들은 죽음을 무서워하지 않는다.

9 This d_________________ can be cured completely.
이 질병은 완전히 치료될 수 있다.

10 He e_________________ how to grow corn.
그는 옥수수를 기르는 방법을 설명했다.

Review에서 틀린 문제의 영어 단어와 우리말 뜻을 쓴 다음, 영어 단어를 3번씩 쓰세요.

	( )	_________ _________ _________
	( )	_________ _________ _________
	( )	_________ _________ _________
	( )	_________ _________ _________
	( )	_________ _________ _________

01 broad
[brɔːd]

형 넓은
They swam across a broad river.
그들은 넓은 강을 헤엄쳐 건넜다.

02 compare
[kəmpɛ́ər]

동 비교하다
Andy compared the two animals carefully.
Andy는 그 두 동물들을 신중하게 비교했다.

03 deep
[diːp]

형 깊은
The coin fell into the deep pond.
그 동전은 깊은 연못에 빠졌다.

04 giant
[dʒáiənt]

형 거대한
He is making a giant statue.
그는 거대한 조각상을 만들고 있다.

05 gram
[græm]

명 (단위) 그램
I should eat five grams of salt a day.
나는 하루에 소금을 5그램 먹어야 한다.

06 half
[hæf]

명 절반　✿ in half 절반으로
The kid cut the apple in half.
그 아이는 그 사과를 반으로 잘랐다.

07 height
[hait]

명 높이, 키
The two towers are equal in height.
그 두 개의 탑은 높이가 동일하다.

08 high
[hai]

형 높은　부 높이
The stairs are too high.
그 계단은 너무 높다.

09 huge
[hjuːdʒ]

형 엄청난, 거대한
A huge bone was found in the desert.
거대한 뼈 하나가 사막에서 발견되었다.

10 kilogram
[kíləgræm]

명 (단위) 킬로그램
The bear weighs 150 kilograms.
그 곰은 몸무게가 150킬로그램이다.

Daily Test

A 우리말 뜻과 일치하도록 빠진 글자를 써넣어 단어를 완성하세요.

1 깊은   __ e __ __ __   **2** 엄청난, 거대한   __ __ __ e

3 높이, 키   __ __ __ g __ t   **4** (단위) 그램   __ r __ m

5 절반   h __ __ __

B 다음 영어 단어의 우리말 뜻을 쓰세요.

1 high   _________________   **2** kilogram   _________________

3 broad   _________________   **4** compare   _________________

5 giant   _________________

C 우리말 뜻과 일치하도록 빈칸에 알맞은 단어를 써넣어 문장을 완성하세요.

1 They swam across a _________________ river.
그들은 넓은 강을 헤엄쳐 건넜다.

2 The bear weighs 150 _________________.
그 곰은 몸무게가 150킬로그램이다.

3 Andy _________________ the two animals carefully.
Andy는 그 두 동물들을 신중하게 비교했다.

4 The kid cut the apple in _________________.
그 아이는 그 사과를 반으로 잘랐다.

5 The coin fell into the _________________ pond.
그 동전은 깊은 연못에 빠졌다.

6 The stairs are too _________________.
그 계단은 너무 높다.

7 I should eat five _________________ of salt a day.
나는 하루에 소금을 5그램 먹어야 한다.

8 The two towers are equal in _________________.
그 두 개의 탑은 높이가 동일하다.

11 kilometer
[kilámitər]

명 (단위) 킬로미터
He drives 30 kilometers to work.
그는 직장까지 30킬로미터를 운전한다.

12 large
[lɑːrdʒ]

형 큰
The museum is not large, is it?
그 박물관은 크지 않아, 그렇지?

13 long
[lɔ(ː)ŋ]

형 긴
How long is the elephant's nose?
그 코끼리의 코는 얼마나 기니?

14 meter
[míːtər]

명 (단위) 미터
The woman ran 100 meters in 15 seconds.
그 여자는 100미터를 15초에 달렸다.

15 narrow
[nǽrou]

형 좁은
The narrow trail leads to the falls.
그 좁은 오솔길은 폭포로 이어진다.

16 scale
[skeil]

명 규모, 범위
The performance was held on a big scale.
그 공연은 큰 규모로 열렸다.

17 size
[saiz]

명 크기
Those jars are different in size.
저 병들은 크기가 다르다.

18 small
[smɔːl]

형 작은
We were born in a small town.
우리는 작은 도시에서 태어났다.

19 tiny
[táini]

형 매우 작은
It is hard to catch the tiny bugs.
그 매우 작은 벌레들을 잡는 것은 어렵다.

20 wide
[waid]

형 넓은
I looked out the wide window.
나는 그 넓은 창 밖을 내다보았다.

A 우리말 뜻과 일치하도록 빠진 글자를 써넣어 단어를 완성하세요.

1 긴   __ o __ __

2 작은   __ __ __ l __

3 넓은   __ __ d __

4 큰   __ a __ g __

5 (단위) 미터   __ __ t __ r

B 다음 영어 단어의 우리말 뜻을 쓰세요.

1 scale   ________________

2 kilometer   ________________

3 tiny   ________________

4 narrow   ________________

5 size   ________________

C 우리말 뜻과 일치하도록 빈칸에 알맞은 단어를 써넣어 문장을 완성하세요.

1 The ________________ trail leads to the falls.
그 좁은 오솔길은 폭포로 이어진다.

2 The performance was held on a big ________________.
그 공연은 큰 규모로 열렸다.

3 The woman ran 100 ________________ in 15 seconds.
그 여자는 100미터를 15초에 달렸다.

4 How ________________ is the elephant's nose?
그 코끼리의 코는 얼마나 기니?

5 I looked out the ________________ window.
나는 그 넓은 창 밖을 내다보았다.

6 It is hard to catch the ________________ bugs.
그 매우 작은 벌레들을 잡는 것은 어렵다.

7 He drives 30 ________________ to work.
그는 직장까지 30킬로미터를 운전한다.

8 We were born in a ________________ town.
우리는 작은 도시에서 태어났다.

01 accident [ǽksidənt]
명 사고
I saw a car accident yesterday.
나는 어제 자동차 사고를 봤다.

02 alive [əláiv]
형 살아 있는
My grandparents are still alive.
나의 조부모님은 아직 살아 계신다.

03 ambulance [ǽmbjələns]
명 구급차
The patient was waiting for an ambulance.
그 환자는 구급차를 기다리고 있었다.

04 blind [blaind]
형 눈이 먼, 시각 장애가 있는
The man was slowly going blind.
그 남자는 천천히 눈이 멀어가고 있었다.

05 careful [kέərfəl]
형 조심하는, 주의 깊은
I am a very careful driver.
나는 매우 조심성 있는 운전자이다.

06 damage [dǽmidʒ]
명 손상, 피해 동 훼손하다 ✿ do damage 피해를 주다
The storm did a lot of damage to the house.
그 폭풍우는 그 집에 많은 피해를 주었다.

07 danger [déindʒər]
명 위험
The travelers were in great danger then.
그 여행자들은 그때 큰 위험에 처해 있었다.

08 deaf [def]
형 귀가 먹은, 청각 장애가 있는
Deaf people use sign language.
청각 장애인들은 수화를 사용한다.

09 emergency [imə́:rdʒənsi]
명 비상 (사태)
The emergency exit is at the end of the aisle.
비상구는 통로 끝에 있다.

10 escape [iskéip]
동 달아나다, 탈출하다
The family escaped from the building.
그 가족은 그 건물에서 탈출했다.

A 우리말 뜻과 일치하도록 빠진 글자를 써넣어 단어를 완성하세요.

1 위험   __ a __ g __ __ __   2 살아있는   __ __ __ v e

3 사고   __ c __ __ d __ __ t   4 달아나다, 탈출하다 __ __ c __ p __

5 조심하는, 주의 깊은   __ a r __ __ __ __

B 다음 영어 단어의 우리말 뜻을 쓰세요.

1 deaf   _________________   2 blind   _________________

3 damage   _________________   4 emergency   _________________

5 ambulance   _________________

C 우리말 뜻과 일치하도록 빈칸에 알맞은 단어를 써넣어 문장을 완성하세요.

1 The storm did a lot of _________________ to the house.
그 폭풍우는 그 집에 많은 피해를 주었다.

2 The family _________________ from the building.
그 가족은 그 건물에서 탈출했다.

3 The patient was waiting for an _________________.
그 환자는 구급차를 기다리고 있었다.

4 The man was slowly going _________________.
그 남자는 천천히 눈이 멀어가고 있었다.

5 The travelers were in great _________________ then.
그 여행자들은 그때 큰 위험에 처해 있었다.

6 _________________ people use sign language.
청각 장애인들은 수화를 사용한다.

7 My grandparents are still _________________.
나의 조부모님은 아직 살아 계신다.

8 I saw a car _________________ yesterday.
나는 어제 자동차 사그를 봤다.

11 happen
[hǽpən]

동 발생하다, 일어나다
When did it happen?
그것은 언제 일어났나요?

12 harm
[hɑːrm]

명 해, 피해 동 해치다
The guy didn't harm the boy.
그 남자는 그 소년을 해치지 않았다.

13 injured
[índʒərd]

형 부상을 입은, 다친
The nurse took care of the injured kids.
그 간호사는 그 다친 아이들을 돌보았다.

14 pain
[pein]

명 아픔, 통증
He was suffering from chest pain.
그는 가슴 통증으로 고통받고 있었다.

15 prevent
[privént]

동 막다, 예방하다
We have to try to prevent fire.
우리는 화재를 예방하기 위해 노력해야 한다.

16 safe
[seif]

형 안전한
The children feel safe in the school.
그 어린이들은 학교에서 안전하다고 느낀다.

17 safety
[séifti]

명 안전
For safety, don't go out at night.
안전을 위해, 밤에는 나가지 마.

18 save
[seiv]

동 구하다
The hero saved the baby's life.
그 영웅은 그 아기의 생명을 구했다.

19 survive
[sərváiv]

동 살아남다, 생존하다
The big animal survived in the desert.
그 큰 동물은 사막에서 살아남았다.

20 traffic
[trǽfik]

명 차량들, 교통(량)
I was stuck in a traffic jam.
나는 교통 체증에 걸렸다.

A 우리말 뜻과 일치하도록 빠진 글자를 써넣어 단어를 완성하세요.

1 안전한   __ __ f __   2 해, 피해; 해치다   __ __ __ m

3 구하다   s __ __ __   4 아픔, 통증   __ __ i __

5 살아남다, 생존하다 __ __ __ v __ __ e

B 다음 영어 단어의 우리말 뜻을 쓰세요.

1 prevent ________________   2 happen ________________

3 traffic ________________   4 injured ________________

5 safety ________________

C 우리말 뜻과 일치하도록 빈칸에 알맞은 단어를 써넣어 문장을 완성하세요.

1 We have to try to ________________ fire.
우리는 화재를 예방하기 위해 노력해야 한다.

2 When did it ________________?
그것은 언제 일어났나요?

3 He was suffering from chest ________________.
그는 가슴 통증으로 고통받고 있었다.

4 The big animal ________________ in the desert.
그 큰 동물은 사막에서 살아남았다.

5 The guy didn't ________________ the boy.
그 남자는 그 소년을 해치지 않았다.

6 For ________________, don't go out at night.
안전을 위해, 밤에는 나가지 마.

7 The hero ________________ the baby's life.
그 영웅은 그 아기의 생명을 구했다.

8 The nurse took care of the ________________ kids.
그 간호사는 그 다친 아이들을 돌보았다.

01 birthday
[bə́ːrθdèi]

® 명 생일
I will wear the dress for my birthday party.
나는 나의 생일 파티에서 그 드레스를 입을 것이다.

02 date
[deit]

® 명 날짜
What's the date today?
오늘은 며칠이니?

03 day
[dei]

® 명 하루, 날, 요일
I met Emily three days ago.
나는 3일 전에 Emily를 만났다.

04 fall
[fɔːl]

® 명 가을
We will go on a trip to Japan this fall.
우리는 이번 가을에 일본으로 여행을 갈 것이다.

05 Friday
[fráidei]

® 명 금요일
Are you busy next Friday?
너는 다음 금요일에 바쁘니?

06 Monday
[mʌ́ndei]

® 명 월요일
I thought today was Monday.
나는 오늘이 월요일이라고 생각했다.

07 Saturday
[sǽtərdèi]

® 명 토요일
Who will go fishing this Saturday?
누가 이번 토요일에 낚시를 하러 갈 거니?

08 season
[síːzən]

® 명 계절
We have four seasons in Korea.
한국에는 사계절이 있다.

09 spring
[spriŋ]

® 명 봄
It is windy here in spring.
여기는 봄에 바람이 많이 분다.

10 summer
[sʌ́mər]

® 명 여름
The country is really hot in summer.
그 나라는 여름에 정말 덥다.

A 우리말 뜻과 일치하도록 빠진 글자를 써넣어 단어를 완성하세요.

1 날짜   __ __ t __

2 여름   __ u m __ __ __

3 월요일   __ __ __ __ a y

4 계절   __ e __ __ __ n

5 토요일   __ __ __ __ __ d a y

B 다음 영어 단어의 우리말 뜻을 쓰세요.

1 day   ________________

2 fall   ________________

3 spring   ________________

4 birthday   ________________

5 Friday   ________________

C 우리말 뜻과 일치하도록 빈칸에 알맞은 단어를 써넣어 문장을 완성하세요.

1 We have four ________________ in Korea.
한국에는 사계절이 있다.

2 We will go on a trip to Japan this ________________.
우리는 이번 가을에 일본으로 여행을 갈 것이다.

3 It is windy here in ________________.
여기는 봄에 바람이 많이 분다.

4 I thought today was ________________.
나는 오늘이 월요일이라고 생각했다.

5 Are you busy next ________________?
너는 다음 금요일에 바쁘니?

6 I will wear the dress for my ________________ party.
나는 나의 생일 파티에서 그 드레스를 입을 것이다.

7 The country is really hot in ________________.
그 나라는 여름에 정말 덥다.

8 Who will go fishing this ________________?
누가 이번 토요일에 낚시를 하러 갈 거니?

11 Sunday
[sʌ́ndei]

몡 일요일
The mall will have a sale this Sunday.
그 쇼핑몰은 이번 일요일에 할인 판매를 할 것이다.

12 Thursday
[θə́:rzdei]

몡 목요일
There are no yoga classes on Thursday.
목요일에는 요가 수업이 없다.

13 today
[tədéi]

뿐 몡 오늘
I have a lot of time today.
나는 오늘 시간이 많다.

14 tomorrow
[təmɔ́:rou]

뿐 몡 내일
What is our schedule for tomorrow?
우리의 내일 일정은 무엇이니?

15 Tuesday
[tjú:zdei]

몡 화요일
He will be back before next Tuesday.
그는 다음 화요일 전에 돌아올 것이다.

16 Wednesday
[wénzdei]

몡 수요일
Are you free for dinner on Wednesday?
너는 수요일에 저녁 식사를 함께 할 시간이 있니?

17 week
[wi:k]

몡 주, 일주일
The singer stays in this city for a week.
그 가수는 일주일 동안 이 도시에 머무른다.

18 weekend
[wí:kènd]

몡 주말
My weekend plan is camping in the forest.
나의 주말 계획은 숲에서 캠핑을 하는 것이다.

19 winter
[wíntər]

몡 겨울
Does he enjoy skiing in winter?
그는 겨울에 스키를 즐기니?

20 yesterday
[jéstərdei]

뿐 몡 어제
The students had a test yesterday.
그 학생들은 어제 시험을 봤다.

A 우리말 뜻과 일치하도록 빠진 글자를 써넣어 단어를 완성하세요.

1 겨울 __ i n __ __ __

2 목요일 __ __ __ __ s d a y

3 오늘 __ __ __ a y

4 화요일 __ __ __ __ d a y

5 어제 y __ __ t __ __ d __ __

B 다음 영어 단어의 우리말 뜻을 쓰세요.

1 tomorrow ________________

2 Wednesday ________________

3 weekend ________________

4 Sunday ________________

5 week ________________

C 우리말 뜻과 일치하도록 빈칸에 알맞은 단어를 써넣어 문장을 완성하세요.

1 I have a lot of time ________________.
나는 오늘 시간이 많다.

2 Are you free for dinner on ________________?
너는 수요일에 저녁 식사를 함께 할 시간이 있니?

3 There are no yoga classes on ________________.
목요일에는 요가 수업이 없다.

4 He will be back before next ________________.
그는 다음 화요일 전에 돌아올 것이다.

5 My ________________ plan is camping in the forest.
나의 주말 계획은 숲에서 캠핑을 하는 것이다.

6 The mall will have a sale this ________________.
그 쇼핑몰은 이번 일요일에 할인 판매를 할 것이다.

7 The students had a test ________________.
그 학생들은 어제 시험을 봤다.

8 Does he enjoy skiing in ________________?
그는 겨울에 스키를 즐기니?

Day 24_01

01	**dust** [dʌst]	명 먼지 The coat is covered with dust. 그 코트는 먼지로 덮여 있다.
02	**earthquake** [ə́ːrθkwèik]	명 지진 A big earthquake hit China a few years ago. 몇 년 전에 큰 지진이 중국을 강타했다.
03	**fire** [faiər]	명 불, 화재 They collect branches to make fire. 그들은 불을 만들기 위해 나뭇가지들을 모은다.
04	**flood** [flʌd]	명 홍수 I read an article about the flood. 나는 그 홍수에 관한 기사를 읽었다.
05	**forecast** [fɔ́ːrkæst]	명 예측　동 예측하다　✿ weather forecast 일기 예보 Listen to the weather forecast carefully. 일기 예보를 주의 깊게 들어.
06	**freeze** [friːz]	동 얼다, 얼리다　✿ freeze-froze-frozen Water freezes at 0℃. 물은 섭씨 0도에서 언다.
07	**heat** [hiːt]	명 열, 더위 I can't stand the heat of summer. 나는 여름의 더위를 견딜 수 없다.
08	**hurricane** [hə́ːrəkèin]	명 허리케인 Many people died because of the hurricane. 그 허리케인 때문에 많은 사람들이 죽었다.
09	**ice** [ais]	명 얼음 Why don't we skate on the ice? 얼음 위에서 스케이트를 타는 게 어때?
10	**lightning** [láitniŋ]	명 번개, 번갯불 Lightning flashed in the sky. 하늘에서 번개가 번쩍였다.

Daily Test

A 우리말 뜻과 일치하도록 빠진 글자를 써넣어 단어를 완성하세요.

1 얼다, 얼리다   _ _ e _ z _

2 먼지   _ u _ _

3 열, 더위   _ _ _ t

4 홍수   _ _ o o _

5 번개, 번갯불   _ _ g h _ _ i _ g

B 다음 영어 단어의 우리말 뜻을 쓰세요.

1 earthquake _________________

2 forecast _________________

3 ice _________________

4 hurricane _________________

5 fire _________________

C 우리말 뜻과 일치하도록 빈칸에 알맞은 단어를 써넣어 문장을 완성하세요.

1 I read an article about the _________________.
나는 그 홍수에 관한 기사를 읽었다.

2 Many people died because of the _________________.
그 허리케인 때문에 많은 사람들이 죽었다.

3 A big _________________ hit China a few years ago.
몇 년 전에 큰 지진이 중국을 강타했다.

4 The coat is covered with _________________.
그 코트는 먼지로 덮여 있다.

5 Why don't we skate on the _________________?
얼음 위에서 스케이트를 타는 게 어때?

6 They collect branches to make _________________.
그들은 불을 만들기 위해 나뭇가지들을 모은다.

7 _________________ flashed in the sky.
하늘에서 번개가 번쩍였다.

8 Water _________________ at 0°C.
물은 섭씨 0도에서 언다.

11 melt
[melt]
동 녹다, 녹이다
The snow finally began to melt.
눈이 드디어 녹기 시작했다.

12 nature
[néitʃər]
명 자연
The photo shows the beauty of nature.
그 사진은 자연의 아름다움을 보여 준다.

13 rainbow
[réinbòu]
명 무지개
The rainbow was clear and beautiful.
그 무지개는 선명하고 아름다웠다.

14 shower
[ʃáuər]
명 소나기
I waited until the shower passed.
나는 그 소나기가 지나갈 때까지 기다렸다.

15 sunlight
[sʌ́nlàit]
명 햇빛, 햇살
The bright sunlight woke me up.
그 밝은 햇빛이 나를 깨웠다.

16 temperature
[témpərətʃər]
명 온도, 기온
What was the highest temperature today?
오늘 최고 기온은 얼마였니?

17 thunder
[θʌ́ndər]
명 천둥, 우레
He was surprised by the sudden thunder.
그는 갑작스러운 천둥에 놀랐다.

18 typhoon
[taifúːn]
명 태풍
A typhoon struck the island.
태풍이 그 섬을 강타했다.

19 volcano
[vɑlkéinou]
명 화산
The plant grows only around the volcano.
그 식물은 그 화산 주변에서만 자란다.

20 weather
[wéðər]
명 날씨
The weather is getting warmer day by day.
날씨가 나날이 따뜻해지고 있다.

Daily Test

A 우리말 뜻과 일치하도록 빠진 글자를 써넣어 단어를 완성하세요.

1 천둥, 우레   _ _ u _ d _ _   **2** 소나기   _ h o _ _ _ _

3 녹다, 녹이다   _ _ _ t   **4** 화산   _ o _ _ _ n _

5 햇빛, 햇살   _ u _ l _ _ h _

B 다음 영어 단어의 우리말 뜻을 쓰세요.

1 nature   _________________   **2** weather   _________________

3 temperature   _________________   **4** typhoon   _________________

5 rainbow   _________________

C 우리말 뜻과 일치하도록 빈칸에 알맞은 단어를 써넣어 문장을 완성하세요.

1 He was surprised by the sudden _________________.
그는 갑작스러운 천둥에 놀랐다.

2 What was the highest _________________ today?
오늘 최고 기온은 얼마였니?

3 The _________________ is getting warmer day by day.
날씨가 나날이 따뜻해지고 있다.

4 A _________________ struck the island.
태풍이 그 섬을 강타했다.

5 The _________________ was clear and beautiful.
그 무지개는 선명하고 아름다웠다.

6 The snow finally began to _________________.
눈이 드디어 녹기 시작했다.

7 I waited until the _________________ passed.
나는 그 소나기가 지나갈 때까지 기다렸다.

8 The bright _________________ woke me up.
그 밝은 햇빛이 나를 깨웠다.

A 우리말 뜻에 해당하는 영어 단어를 찾아 동그라미 하세요.

| 살아 있는 | 작은 | 오늘 | 불, 화재 | (단위) 그램 |
| 구하다 | 여름 | 아픔, 통증 | 긴 | 녹다, 녹이다 |

z	x	m	e	l	t	s	h	z	j
f	s	w	r	t	o	l	a	j	s
i	u	t	n	p	d	m	g	v	d
r	m	r	c	w	a	h	g	q	e
e	m	d	t	r	y	g	q	y	p
t	e	p	g	k	w	s	z	d	a
n	r	g	s	m	a	l	l	p	i
a	l	i	v	e	l	o	n	g	n

B 우리말 뜻과 일치하도록 알맞은 단어를 골라 문장을 완성하세요.

| days | giant | tomorrow | forecast | nature | emergency |

1 Listen to the weather ________________ carefully.
일기 예보를 주의 깊게 들어.

2 The ________________ exit is at the end of the aisle.
비상구는 통로 끝에 있다.

3 He is making a ________________ statue.
그는 거대한 조각상을 만들고 있다.

4 What is our schedule for ________________?
우리의 내일 일정은 무엇이니?

5 The photo shows the beauty of ________________.
그 사진은 자연의 아름다움을 보여 준다.

6 I met Emily three ________________ ago.
나는 3일 전에 Emily를 만났다.

C 들려 주는 영어 단어를 바르게 쓴 다음, 우리말 뜻을 써넣으세요.

Day 25_C

	영어 단어	우리말		영어 단어	우리말
1			11		
2			12		
3			13		
4			14		
5			15		
6			16		
7			17		
8			18		
9			19		
10			20		

D 우리말 뜻과 일치하도록 알맞은 단어를 골라 동그라미 하세요.

1 Those jars are different in (scale / size).
저 병들은 크기가 다르다.

2 The children feel (safe / deaf) in the school.
그 어린이들은 학교에서 안전하다고 느낀다.

3 The plant grows only around the (thunder / volcano).
그 식물은 그 화산 주변에서만 자란다.

4 A (huge / deep) bone was found in the desert.
거대한 뼈 하나가 사막에서 발견되었다.

5 I am a very (injured / careful) driver.
나는 매우 조심성 있는 운전자이다.

6 It is windy here in (spring / fall).
여기는 봄에 바람이 많이 분다.

E 영어는 우리말로, 우리말은 영어로 바꿔 쓰세요.

1	happen	__________	2 구급차	__________
3	Tuesday	__________	4 (단위) 킬로미터	__________
5	compare	__________	6 일요일	__________
7	dust	__________	8 안전	__________
9	deaf	__________	10 허리케인	__________
11	lightning	__________	12 생일	__________
13	harm	__________	14 절반	__________
15	narrow	__________	16 주말	__________
17	shower	__________	18 매우 작은	__________
19	Monday	__________	20 천둥, 우레	__________

Day 25_F

F 잘 듣고, 빈칸에 알맞은 단어를 써넣어 문장을 완성하세요.

1 A ________________ struck the island.

2 I looked out the ________________ window.

3 Does he enjoy skiing in ________________?

4 We have to try to ________________ fire.

5 Are you busy next ________________?

6 I read an article about the ________________.

7 The storm did a lot of ________________ to the house.

8 The bear weighs 150 ________________.

G 우리말 뜻과 일치하도록 빈칸에 알맞은 단어를 써넣어 문장을 완성하세요.

1 A big e________________ hit China a few years ago.
몇 년 전에 큰 지진이 중국을 강타했다.

2 The museum is not l________________, is it?
그 박물관은 크지 않아, 그렇지?

3 Who will go fishing this S________________?
누가 이번 토요일에 낚시를 하러 갈 거니?

4 I was stuck in a t________________ jam.
나는 교통 체증에 걸렸다.

5 I can't stand the h________________ of summer.
나는 여름의 더위를 견딜 수 없다.

6 The singer stays in this city for a w________________.
그 가수는 일주일 동안 이 도시에 머무른다.

7 The two towers are equal in h________________.
그 두 개의 탑은 높이가 동일하다.

8 The family e________________ from the building.
그 가족은 그 건물에서 탈출했다.

9 What's the d________________ today?
오늘은 며칠이니?

10 The bright s________________ woke me up.
그 밝은 햇빛이 나를 깨웠다.

Review에서 틀린 문제의 영어 단어와 우리말 뜻을 쓴 다음, 영어 단어를 3번씩 쓰세요.

	( )		
	( )		
	( )		
	( )		
	( )		

01 active
[ǽktiv]

형 활동적인, 활발한
The children were active during the class.
그 어린이들은 수업 중에 활발했다.

02 brave
[breiv]

형 용감한
The brave young man caught a thief.
그 용감한 젊은이는 도둑을 잡았다.

03 cheerful
[tʃíərfəl]

형 발랄한, 쾌활한
Everyone likes the cheerful girl.
모든 사람이 그 쾌활한 소녀를 좋아한다.

04 clever
[klévər]

형 영리한, 똑똑한
I'm proud of my clever daughter.
나는 나의 똑똑한 딸이 자랑스럽다.

05 confident
[kánfidənt]

형 자신감 있는
She talked in a confident voice.
그녀는 자신감 있는 목소리로 말했다.

06 courage
[kə́:ridʒ]

명 용기
He had courage to do the right thing.
그는 옳은 일을 할 용기가 있었다.

07 curious
[kjú(:)əriəs]

형 호기심이 많은
The curious boy asks a lot of questions.
그 호기심 많은 소년은 질문을 많이 한다.

08 gentle
[dʒéntl]

형 온화한, 순한
The teacher always looks gentle.
그 선생님은 항상 온화해 보인다.

09 honest
[ánist]

형 정직한, 솔직한   ✿ to be honest 솔직히 말하면
To be honest, it was my mistake.
솔직히 말하면, 그것은 나의 실수였다.

10 kind
[kaind]

형 친절한, 다정한
The kind woman rarely says no.
그 친절한 여자는 아니라고 거의 말하지 않는다.

Daily Test

A 우리말 뜻과 일치하도록 빠진 글자를 써넣어 단어를 완성하세요.

1 영리한, 똑똑한   __ l __ __ __ r   **2** 용감한   __ r __ v __

3 친절한, 다정한   __ __ n __   **4** 호기심이 많은   __ __ r __ __ u s

5 활동적인, 활발한   __ __ __ __ v e

B 다음 영어 단어의 우리말 뜻을 쓰세요.

1 confident   __________________   **2** honest   __________________

3 gentle   __________________   **4** cheerful   __________________

5 courage   __________________

C 우리말 뜻과 일치하도록 빈칸에 알맞은 단어를 써넣어 문장을 완성하세요.

1 The __________________ woman rarely says no.
그 친절한 여자는 아니라고 거의 말하지 않는다.

2 I'm proud of my __________________ daughter.
나는 나의 똑똑한 딸이 자랑스럽다.

3 Everyone likes the __________________ girl.
모든 사람이 그 쾌활한 소녀를 좋아한다.

4 The __________________ young man caught a thief.
그 용감한 젊은이는 도둑을 잡았다.

5 She talked in a __________________ voice.
그녀는 자신감 있는 목소리로 말했다.

6 The children were __________________ during the class.
그 어린이들은 수업 중에 활발했다.

7 The __________________ boy asks a lot of questions.
그 호기심 많은 소년은 질문을 많이 한다.

8 He had __________________ to do the right thing.
그는 옳은 일을 할 용기가 있었다.

11 lazy
[léizi]

형 게으른
The lazy man is often late for an appointment.
그 게으른 남자는 자주 약속에 늦는다.

12 mean
[mi:n]

형 못된, 심술궂은
Don't be so mean to your friends!
너의 친구들에게 너무 못되게 굴지 마!

13 mild
[maild]

형 온화한, 순한
All the kids love her mild smile.
그 모든 아이들은 그녀의 온화한 미소를 사랑한다.

14 passion
[pǽʃən]

명 열정
We admire his passion for learning.
우리는 배움에 대한 그의 열정을 존경한다.

15 quiet
[kwáiət]

형 조용한, 차분한
The student is quiet and diligent.
그 학생은 조용하고 성실하다.

16 selfish
[sélfiʃ]

형 이기적인
I regret my selfish behavior.
나는 나의 이기적인 행동을 후회한다.

17 silly
[síli]

형 어리석은, 바보 같은
Don't be silly!
바보 같이 굴지 마!

18 smart
[smɑ:rt]

형 똑똑한, 영리한
The smart man passed the test at once.
그 똑똑한 남자는 그 시험을 한 번에 통과했다.

19 talkative
[tɔ́:kətiv]

형 수다스러운
I don't like him because he is too talkative.
나는 그가 너무 수다스러워서 그를 좋아하지 않는다.

20 wise
[waiz]

형 현명한, 지혜로운
Who is the wisest in this group?
이 그룹에서 누가 가장 현명하니?

Daily Test

A 우리말 뜻과 일치하도록 빠진 글자를 써넣어 단어를 완성하세요.

1 조용한, 차분한 　＿ u ＿ ＿ ＿ **2** 어리석은, 바보 같은 　＿ ＿ ＿ l y

3 열정 　＿ ＿ s ＿ i ＿ ＿ **4** 현명한, 지혜로운 　w ＿ ＿ ＿

5 게으른 　＿ a ＿ ＿

B 다음 영어 단어의 우리말 뜻을 쓰세요.

1 smart ＿＿＿＿＿＿＿＿ **2** mean ＿＿＿＿＿＿＿＿

3 selfish ＿＿＿＿＿＿＿＿ **4** talkative ＿＿＿＿＿＿＿＿

5 mild ＿＿＿＿＿＿＿＿

C 우리말 뜻과 일치하도록 빈칸에 알맞은 단어를 써넣어 문장을 완성하세요.

1 The ＿＿＿＿＿＿＿＿ man is often late for an appointment.
그 게으른 남자는 자주 약속에 늦는다.

2 The student is ＿＿＿＿＿＿＿＿ and diligent.
그 학생은 조용하고 성실하다.

3 Don't be so ＿＿＿＿＿＿＿＿ to your friends!
너의 친구들에게 너무 못되게 굴지 마!

4 All the kids love her ＿＿＿＿＿＿＿＿ smile.
그 모든 아이들은 그녀의 온화한 미소를 사랑한다.

5 Don't be ＿＿＿＿＿＿＿＿!
바보 같이 굴지 마!

6 I don't like him because he is too ＿＿＿＿＿＿＿＿.
나는 그가 너무 수다스러워서 그를 좋아하지 않는다.

7 I regret my ＿＿＿＿＿＿＿＿ behavior.
나는 나의 이기적인 행동을 후회한다.

8 We admire his ＿＿＿＿＿＿＿＿ for learning.
우리는 배움에 대한 그의 열정을 존경한다.

01 announcer
[ənáunsər]

🐤 명 아나운서
The announcer has a soft voice.
그 아나운서는 부드러운 목소리를 가지고 있다.

02 architect
[á:rkitèkt]

🐤 명 건축가
She wants to be an architect.
그녀는 건축가가 되기를 원한다.

03 astronaut
[ǽstrənɔ̀:t]

🐤 명 우주 비행사
Astronauts also feel scared.
우주 비행사들도 두려움을 느낀다.

04 athlete
[ǽθli:t]

🐤 명 운동선수
The athlete is training now.
그 운동선수는 지금 훈련을 하고 있다.

05 author
[ɔ́:θər]

🐤 명 작가, 저자
The author writes his books in a quiet place.
그 작가는 조용한 장소에서 그의 책을 쓴다.

06 bodyguard
[bádigà:rd]

🐤 명 경호원, 보디가드
The actor is guarded by a bodyguard.
그 배우는 경호원에게 보호받는다.

07 carpenter
[ká:rpəntər]

🐤 명 목수
The carpenter is using a hammer.
그 목수는 망치를 사용하고 있다.

08 chef
[ʃef]

🐤 명 요리사
He works as a chef in the hotel.
그는 그 호텔에서 요리사로 일한다.

09 dentist
[déntist]

🐤 명 치과 의사
The dentist told me to open my mouth.
그 치과 의사는 나에게 입을 벌리라고 말했다.

10 detective
[ditéktiv]

🐤 명 형사
The detective found new evidence.
그 형사는 새로운 증거를 발견했다.

Daily Test

A 우리말 뜻과 일치하도록 빠진 글자를 써넣어 단어를 완성하세요.

1 작가, 저자   _ u _ _ o _

2 요리사   _ h _ _

3 운동선수   _ _ _ l _ t _

4 치과 의사   d _ _ t _ _ _

5 아나운서   _ n n _ _ _ c _ r

B 다음 영어 단어의 우리말 뜻을 쓰세요.

1 detective   ___________________

2 carpenter   ___________________

3 architect   ___________________

4 bodyguard   ___________________

5 astronaut   ___________________

C 우리말 뜻과 일치하도록 빈칸에 알맞은 단어를 써넣어 문장을 완성하세요.

1 ___________________ also feel scared.
우주 비행사들도 두려움을 느낀다.

2 The ___________________ is using a hammer.
그 목수는 망치를 사용하고 있다.

3 The ___________________ found new evidence.
그 형사는 새로운 증거를 발견했다.

4 She wants to be an ___________________.
그녀는 건축가가 되기를 원한다.

5 He works as a ___________________ in the hotel.
그는 그 호텔에서 요리사로 일한다.

6 The ___________________ is training now.
그 운동선수는 지금 훈련을 하고 있다.

7 The ___________________ has a soft voice.
그 아나운서는 부드러운 목소리를 가지고 있다.

8 The ___________________ writes his books in a quiet place.
그 작가는 조용한 장소에서 그의 책을 쓴다.

11 engineer
[èndʒəníər]

명 엔지니어, 기술자
The engineer has excellent skills.
그 엔지니어는 훌륭한 기술을 가지고 있다.

12 firefighter
[fáiərfàitər]

명 소방관
The two firefighters were injured.
그 소방관 두 명은 부상을 입었다.

13 judge
[dʒʌdʒ]

명 판사
He is a very responsible judge.
그는 매우 책임감이 있는 판사이다.

14 lawyer
[lɔ́:jər]

명 변호사
The lawyer helps poor people.
그 변호사는 가난한 사람들을 돕는다.

15 poet
[póuit]

명 시인
The poet was inspired by the river.
그 시인은 그 강에서 영감을 받았다.

16 police officer
[pəlí:sɔ̀(:)fisər]

명 경찰관
Police officers must keep the law.
경찰관은 법을 지켜야 한다.

17 sailor
[séilər]

명 선원, 뱃사람
How many sailors are there in the ship?
그 배에는 선원이 몇 명 있니?

18 soldier
[sóuldʒər]

명 군인
We saw some soldiers on the street.
우리는 거리에서 군인들을 봤다.

19 waiter
[wéitər]

명 종업원, 웨이터
The waiter is wearing a black tie.
그 웨이터는 검은색 넥타이를 매고 있다.

20 zookeeper
[zú:kì:pər]

명 동물원 사육사
A zookeeper walked to the cage.
동물원 사육사 한 명이 그 우리로 걸어갔다.

Daily Test

A 우리말 뜻과 일치하도록 빠진 글자를 써넣어 단어를 완성하세요.

1 변호사   __ __ w __ __ r

2 종업원, 웨이터   __ a __ __ e r

3 군인   __ __ __ d i __ __

4 판사   j __ d __ __ __

5 선원, 뱃사람   __ a __ __ o __

B 다음 영어 단어의 우리말 뜻을 쓰세요.

1 police officer   ___________________

2 zookeeper   ___________________

3 poet   ___________________

4 engineer   ___________________

5 firefighter   ___________________

C 우리말 뜻과 일치하도록 빈칸에 알맞은 단어를 써넣어 문장을 완성하세요.

1 He is a very responsible ________________.
그는 매우 책임감이 있는 판사이다.

2 The ________________ helps poor people.
그 변호사는 가난한 사람들을 돕는다.

3 The ________________ is wearing a black tie.
그 웨이터는 검은색 넥타이를 매고 있다.

4 The ________________ has excellent skills.
그 엔지니어는 훌륭한 기술을 가지고 있다.

5 A ________________ walked to the cage.
동물원 사육사 한 명이 그 우리로 걸어갔다.

6 The ________________ was inspired by the river.
그 시인은 그 강에서 영감을 받았다.

7 The two ________________ were injured.
그 소방관 두 명은 부상을 입었다.

8 How many ________________ are there in the ship?
그 배에는 선원이 몇 명 있니?

01 appearance
[əpí(:)ərəns]

명 겉모습, 외모
She tries to change her appearance.
그녀는 그녀의 외모를 바꾸려고 노력한다.

02 bald
[bɔːld]

형 대머리의
He isn't ashamed of being bald.
그는 대머리라는 것을 부끄러워하지 않는다.

03 beard
[biərd]

명 (턱)수염
My uncle grows a beard.
나의 삼촌은 턱수염을 기른다.

04 beautiful
[bjúːtəfəl]

형 아름다운
The actresses were very beautiful.
그 여배우들은 매우 아름다웠다.

05 charming
[tʃáːrmiŋ]

형 매력적인
You look charming in this dress.
너는 이 드레스를 입으니 매력적으로 보인다.

06 cheek
[tʃiːk]

명 볼, 뺨
The baby touched me on the cheek.
그 아기는 나의 볼을 만졌다.

07 dimple
[dímpl]

명 보조개
Kathy has dimples when she smiles.
Kathy는 미소 지을 때 보조개가 생긴다.

08 elegant
[éləgənt]

형 우아한
The dancers on TV were elegant.
TV에 나온 무용수들은 우아했다.

09 eyebrow
[áibráu]

명 눈썹
He has thick eyebrows.
그는 눈썹이 짙다.

10 forehead
[fɔ́(:)rhed]

명 이마
A mosquito sat on her forehead.
모기 한 마리가 그녀의 이마 위에 앉았다.

Daily Test

A 우리말 뜻과 일치하도록 빠진 글자를 써넣어 단어를 완성하세요.

1 대머리의   _ _ _ d

2 볼, 뺨   _ _ _ _ _ k

3 눈썹   _ y _ b _ _ _ _

4 (턱)수염   _ _ _ r d

5 매력적인   _ _ a _ m _ _ _

B 다음 영어 단어의 우리말 뜻을 쓰세요.

1 appearance _________________

2 beautiful _________________

3 dimple _________________

4 elegant _________________

5 forehead _________________

C 우리말 뜻과 일치하도록 빈칸에 알맞은 단어를 써넣어 문장을 완성하세요.

1 You look _________________ in this dress.
너는 이 드레스를 입으니 매력적으로 보인다.

2 The dancers on TV were _________________.
TV에 나온 무용수들은 우아했다.

3 A mosquito sat on her _________________.
모기 한 마리가 그녀의 이마 위에 앉았다.

4 My uncle grows a _________________.
나의 삼촌은 턱수염을 기른다.

5 She tries to change her _________________.
그녀는 그녀의 외모를 바꾸려고 노력한다.

6 He isn't ashamed of being _________________.
그는 대머리라는 것을 부끄러워하지 않는다.

7 The actresses were very _________________.
그 여배우들은 매우 아름다웠다.

8 The baby touched me on the _________________.
그 아기는 나의 볼을 만졌다.

11 good-looking
[gùdlúkiŋ]

형 잘생긴
The good-looking man is mad at something.
그 잘생긴 남자는 무언가에 매우 화가 나 있다.

12 gorgeous
[gɔ́ːrdʒəs]

형 아주 멋진
Look at that gorgeous lady.
저 아주 멋진 숙녀를 봐.

13 gum
[gʌm]

명 잇몸
Healthy teeth and gums are important.
건강한 이와 잇몸은 중요하다.

14 jaw
[dʒɔː]

명 턱
The boy has a scar on his jaw.
그 소년은 턱에 흉터가 있다.

15 lip
[lip]

명 입술
The kid had the ice cream on his lips.
그 아이는 입술에 아이스크림이 묻었다.

16 mustache
[mʌ́stæʃ]

명 콧수염
The gentleman loves his mustache.
그 신사는 그의 콧수염을 정말 좋아한다.

17 overweight
[òuvərwéit]

형 과체중의, 비만의
Some overweight people have trouble moving.
어떤 비만인 사람들은 움직이는 데 어려움을 겪는다.

18 stout
[staut]

형 통통한
The pants are for stout men.
그 바지는 통통한 남자들을 위한 것이다.

19 tongue
[tʌŋ]

명 혀
Brushing your tongue is a nice habit.
너의 혀를 닦는 것은 좋은 습관이다.

20 wonderful
[wʌ́ndərfəl]

형 훌륭한
She greeted people with her wonderful manner.
그녀는 훌륭한 태도로 사람들을 맞았다.

Daily Test

1 잇몸   __ u __　　　　**2** 통통한   s __ __ __ t

3 아주 멋진   __ o r __ __ __ __ __ s　　　　**4** 턱   __ __ w

5 훌륭한   __ __ n __ __ r __ __ l

B 다음 영어 단어의 우리말 뜻을 쓰세요.

1 lip   ______________　　　　**2** tongue   ______________

3 mustache   ______________　　　　**4** good-looking   ______________

5 overweight   ______________

C 우리말 뜻과 일치하도록 빈칸에 알맞은 단어를 써넣어 문장을 완성하세요.

1 The boy has a scar on his ______________.
그 소년은 턱에 흉터가 있다.

2 The ______________ man is mad at something.
그 잘생긴 남자는 무언가에 매우 화가 나 있다.

3 Some ______________ people have trouble moving.
어떤 비만인 사람들은 움직이는 데 어려움을 겪는다.

4 She greeted people with her ______________ manner.
그녀는 훌륭한 태도로 사람들을 맞았다.

5 Brushing your ______________ is a nice habit.
너의 혀를 닦는 것은 좋은 습관이다.

6 The pants are for ______________ men.
그 바지는 통통한 남자들을 위한 것이다.

7 The gentleman loves his ______________.
그 신사는 그의 콧수염을 정말 좋아한다.

8 Look at that ______________ lady.
저 아주 멋진 숙녀를 봐.

01 advice
[ədváis]
명 조언, 충고
I need your advice about my presentation.
나는 나의 발표에 관해서 너의 조언이 필요하다.

02 apply
[əplái]
동 지원하다
Does she want to apply for the job?
그녀는 그 일에 지원하고 싶어 하니?

03 boss
[bɑs]
명 상사
My boss is reading the report.
나의 상사는 그 보고서를 읽고 있다.

04 client
[kláiənt]
명 의뢰인, 고객
The client will pay for the chair.
그 고객은 그 의자 비용을 지불할 것이다.

05 company
[kʌ́mpəni]
명 회사
The company is far from the subway station.
그 회사는 지하철역에서 멀리 떨어져 있다.

06 duty
[djúːti]
명 의무, 업무
Pam's duties include managing the team.
Pam의 업무는 그 팀을 관리하는 것을 포함한다.

07 file
[fail]
명 파일, 서류철
You must not lose the file.
너희는 그 파일을 잃어버리면 안 된다.

08 form
[fɔːrm]
명 서식
Filling out this form is not difficult.
이 서식을 작성하는 것은 어렵지 않다.

09 goods
[gudz]
명 상품, 제품
Our goods are less expensive than theirs.
우리의 상품은 그들의 것보다 덜 비싸다.

10 helpful
[hélpfəl]
형 도움이 되는
The research may be helpful.
그 연구가 도움이 될지도 모른다.

Daily Test

A 우리말 뜻과 일치하도록 빠진 글자를 써넣어 단어를 완성하세요.

1 상품, 제품   __ __ o d __   **2** 조언, 충고   __ d __ __ c __

3 의무, 업무   d __ __ __   **4** 의뢰인, 고객   __ __ i __ n __

5 파일, 서류철   __ __ l __

B 다음 영어 단어의 우리말 뜻을 쓰세요.

1 helpful   ________________   **2** apply   ________________

3 boss   ________________   **4** company   ________________

5 form   ________________

C 우리말 뜻과 일치하도록 빈칸에 알맞은 단어를 써넣어 문장을 완성하세요.

1 My ________________ is reading the report.
나의 상사는 그 보고서를 읽고 있다.

2 Our ________________ are less expensive than theirs.
우리의 상품은 그들의 것보다 덜 비싸다.

3 I need your ________________ about my presentation.
나는 나의 발표에 관해서 너의 조언이 필요하다.

4 The ________________ will pay for the chair.
그 고객은 그 의자에 비용을 지불할 것이다.

5 You must not lose the ________________.
너희는 그 파일을 잃어버리면 안 된다.

6 The ________________ is far from the subway station.
그 회사는 지하철역에서 멀리 떨어져 있다.

7 Does she want to ________________ for the job?
그녀는 그 일에 지원하고 싶어 하니?

8 The research may be ________________.
그 연구가 도움이 될지도 모른다.

Day 29 회사

---

11 hire
[haiər]

동 고용하다
They **hired** a new engineer.
그들은 새로운 엔지니어를 고용했다.

---

12 income
[ínkʌm]

명 수입, 소득
His **income** is increasing every month.
그의 수입은 매달 증가하고 있다.

---

13 industry
[índəstri]

명 산업
She works in the car **industry**.
그녀는 자동차 산업에 종사한다.

---

14 offer
[ɔ́(:)fər]

명 제안 동 제안하다
We have to talk about the **offer**.
우리는 그 제안에 대해 이야기해야 한다.

---

15 office
[ɔ́:fis]

명 근무처, 사무실
Where is your **office** located?
너의 사무실은 어디에 위치해 있니?

---

16 project
[prάdʒekt]

명 기획, 프로젝트
Are they interested in this **project**?
그들은 이 프로젝트에 관심이 있니?

---

17 resume
[rézjumèi]

명 이력서
You can send in your **resume** by e-mail.
너는 너의 이력서를 이메일로 보낼 수 있다.

---

18 salary
[sǽləri]

명 급여, 봉급
She saves half of her **salary**.
그녀는 그녀의 급여 중 절반을 저축한다.

---

19 teamwork
[tí:mwə̀:rk]

명 팀워크
We want to improve **teamwork**.
우리는 팀워크를 향상시키기를 원한다.

---

20 work
[wə:rk]

명 일 동 일하다
This **work** needs much effort.
이 일은 많은 노력을 필요로 한다.

Daily Test

A 우리말 뜻과 일치하도록 빠진 글자를 써넣어 단어를 완성하세요.

1 고용하다   __ i __ __

2 수입, 소득   __ n __ __ m __

3 제안; 제안하다   __ __ f __ __

4 근무처, 사무실   __ f __ i __ __

5 팀워크   __ __ __ m w __ __ k

B 다음 영어 단어의 우리말 뜻을 쓰세요.

1 project   __________________

2 industry   __________________

3 work   __________________

4 resume   __________________

5 salary   __________________

C 우리말 뜻과 일치하도록 빈칸에 알맞은 단어를 써넣어 문장을 완성하세요.

1 We want to improve _______________.
우리는 팀워크를 향상시키기를 원한다.

2 They _______________ a new engineer.
그들은 새로운 엔지니어를 고용했다.

3 You can send in your _______________ by e-mail.
너는 너의 이력서를 이메일로 보낼 수 있다.

4 Are they interested in this _______________?
그들은 이 프로젝트에 관심이 있니?

5 We have to talk about the _______________.
우리는 그 제안에 대해 이야기해야 한다.

6 This _______________ needs much effort.
이 일은 많은 노력을 필요로 한다.

7 She saves half of her _______________.
그녀는 그녀의 급여 중 절반을 저축한다.

8 Where is your _______________ located?
너의 사무실은 어디에 위치해 있니?

A 우리말 뜻에 해당하는 영어 단어를 찾아 동그라미 하세요.

대머리의	파일, 서류철	상사	게으른	종업원, 웨이터
요리사	영리한, 똑똑한	일; 일하다	통통한	어리석은, 바보 같은

s	p	t	f	i	l	e	g	z	y
n	t	g	b	p	z	d	q	s	r
c	b	o	s	s	v	w	o	r	k
p	h	c	u	y	r	a	v	z	m
b	p	e	g	t	s	i	l	l	y
a	l	k	f	h	y	t	t	f	r
l	a	z	y	c	l	e	v	e	r
d	p	f	f	d	p	r	g	v	y

B 우리말 뜻과 일치하도록 알맞은 단어를 골라 문장을 완성하세요.

dimples	income	honest	wisest	soldiers	form

1 To be ________________, it was my mistake.
솔직히 말하면, 그것은 나의 실수였다.

2 We saw some ________________ on the street.
우리는 거리에서 군인들을 봤다.

3 Kathy has ________________ when she smiles.
Kathy는 미소 지을 때 보조개가 생긴다.

4 Filling out this ________________ is not difficult.
이 서식을 작성하는 것은 어렵지 않다.

5 Who is the ________________ in this group?
이 그룹에서 누가 가장 현명하니?

6 His ________________ is increasing every month.
그의 수입은 매달 증가하고 있다.

Day 30

Day 30_C

C 들려 주는 영어 단어를 바르게 쓴 다음, 우리말 뜻을 써넣으세요.

	영어 단어	우리말		영어 단어	우리말
1			11		
2			12		
3			13		
4			14		
5			15		
6			16		
7			17		
8			18		
9			19		
10			20		

D 우리말 뜻과 일치하도록 알맞은 단어를 골라 동그라미 하세요.

1 The (smart / cheerful) man passed the test at once.
그 똑똑한 남자는 그 시험을 한 번에 통과했다.

2 The (author / dentist) told me to open my mouth.
그 치과 의사는 나에게 입을 벌리라고 말했다.

3 The kid had the ice cream on his (cheeks / lips).
그 아이는 입술에 아이스크림이 묻었다.

4 Pam's (duties / goods) include managing the team.
Pam의 업무는 그 팀을 관리하는 것을 포함한다.

5 The actor is guarded by a (president / bodyguard).
그 배우는 경호원에게 보호받는다.

6 He has thick (eyebrows / gums).
그는 눈썹이 짙다.

1	announcer	__________	2	이마	__________
3	gorgeous	__________	4	조용한, 차분한	__________
5	brave	__________	6	선원, 뱃사람	__________
7	beard	__________	8	훌륭한	__________
9	project	__________	10	운동선수	__________
11	cheerful	__________	12	고용하다	__________
13	teamwork	__________	14	소방관	__________
15	overweight	__________	16	의뢰인, 고객	__________
17	goods	__________	18	목수	__________
19	mild	__________	20	볼, 뺨	__________

Day 30_F

F 잘 듣고, 빈칸에 알맞은 단어를 써넣어 문장을 완성하세요.

1 He had ______________ to do the right thing.

2 She works in the car ______________.

3 The ______________ found new evidence.

4 Healthy teeth and ______________ are important.

5 I need your ______________ about my presentation.

6 The ______________ helps poor people.

7 I don't like him because he is too ______________.

8 You look ______________ in this dress.

G 우리말 뜻과 일치하도록 빈칸에 알맞은 단어를 써넣어 문장을 완성하세요.

1 We admire his p________________ for learning.
우리는 배움에 대한 그의 열정을 존경한다.

2 She tries to change her a________________.
그녀는 그녀의 외모를 바꾸려고 노력한다.

3 The c________________ is far from the subway station.
그 회사는 지하철역에서 멀리 떨어져 있다.

4 The teacher always looks g________________.
그 선생님은 항상 온화해 보인다.

5 He is a very responsible j________________.
그는 매우 책임감이 있는 판사이다.

6 A________________ also feel scared.
우주 비행사들도 두려움을 느낀다.

7 We have to talk about the o________________.
우리는 그 제안에 대해 이야기해야 한다.

8 The c________________ boy asks a lot of questions.
그 호기심 많은 소년은 질문을 많이 한다.

9 P________________ must keep the law.
경찰관은 법을 지켜야 한다.

10 The gentleman loves his m________________.
그 신사는 그의 콧수염을 정말 좋아한다.

Review에서 틀린 문제의 영어 단어와 우리말 뜻을 쓴 다음, 영어 단어를 3번씩 쓰세요.

Phonics Check

Day 31~35

모르는 단어라서 읽을 수 없다고요?
Phonics를 알면 어떤 단어도 읽을 수 있어요.
Phonics 점검을 통해 영어 자신감을 길러요.

Check! Blends와 묵음을 알면
단어를 쉽게 읽을 수 있어요.

01 black
[blæk]

명 검은색 형 검은
The black T-shirt fits me well.
그 검은색 티셔츠는 나에게 잘 맞는다.

02 blind
[blaind]

형 눈이 먼, 시각 장애가 있는
The blind man is walking with a guide dog.
그 시각 장애인은 안내견과 함께 걷고 있다.

03 block
[blɑk]

동 막다, 차단하다
A huge rock was blocking the street.
거대한 바위 하나가 그 거리를 막고 있었다.

04 blossom
[blɑ́səm]

명 꽃 동 꽃을 피우다
The peach blossom smells sweet.
그 복숭아꽃은 달콤한 냄새가 난다.

05 blow
[blou]

동 불다 ✿ blow-blew-blown ✿ blow out 불어서 끄다
They are blowing out the candles.
그들은 그 초들을 불어서 끄고 있다.

06 clap
[klæp]

동 박수를 치다
Clapping is a way to show respect.
박수를 치는 것은 존경심을 나타내는 방법이다.

07 classroom
[klǽsrù(:)m]

명 교실
He is studying alone in the classroom.
그는 교실에서 혼자 공부를 하고 있다.

08 clean
[kliːn]

동 닦다, 청소하다 형 깨끗한
She always keeps the bathroom clean.
그녀는 항상 욕실을 깨끗하게 유지한다.

09 clerk
[kləːrk]

명 점원
The clerk answered the phone.
그 점원이 그 전화를 받았다.

10 club
[klʌb]

명 클럽, 동호회
She attends the guitar club after work.
그녀는 퇴근 후에 기타 동호회에 참석한다.

Daily Test

A 우리말 뜻과 일치하도록 빠진 글자를 써넣어 단어를 완성하세요.

1 검은색; 검은   __ __ a __ k

2 클럽, 동호회   __ __ u __

3 박수를 치다   __ __ __ p

4 막다, 차단하다   __ __ o c __

5 교실   __ __ a __ __ __ o __ m

B 다음 영어 단어의 우리말 뜻을 쓰세요.

1 blossom ___________________

2 clean ___________________

3 blind ___________________

4 blow ___________________

5 clerk ___________________

C 우리말 뜻과 일치하도록 빈칸에 알맞은 단어를 써넣어 문장을 완성하세요.

1 They are _________________ out the candles.
그들은 그 초들을 불어서 끄고 있다.

2 She attends the guitar _________________ after work.
그녀는 퇴근 후에 기타 동호회에 참석한다.

3 The _________________ T-shirt fits me well.
그 검은색 티셔츠는 나에게 잘 맞는다.

4 He is studying alone in the _________________.
그는 교실에서 혼자 공부를 하고 있다.

5 The _________________ man is walking with a guide dog.
그 시각 장애인은 안내견과 함께 걷고 있다.

6 The _________________ answered the phone.
그 점원이 그 전화를 받았다.

7 A huge rock was _________________ the street.
거대한 바위 하나가 그 거리를 막고 있었다.

8 She always keeps the bathroom _________________.
그녀는 항상 욕실을 깨끗하게 유지한다.

11 flag
[flæg]

명 깃발

Can you raise the flag higher?

너는 그 깃발을 더 높이 들 수 있니?

12 flood
[flʌd]

명 홍수

The flood damaged the town.

그 홍수는 그 도시를 훼손했다.

13 flour
[fláuər]

명 밀가루

Their faces are covered with flour.

그들의 얼굴은 밀가루로 뒤덮여 있다.

14 flower
[fláuər]

명 꽃

The bees are looking for a flower.

그 벌들은 꽃을 찾고 있다.

15 flute
[fluːt]

명 플루트

Bill is playing the flute in the garden.

Bill은 정원에서 플루트를 연주하고 있다.

16 plan
[plæn]

명 계획 동 계획을 세우다

I planned to lose weight.

나는 살을 뺄 계획을 세웠다.

17 plant
[plænt]

명 식물 동 심다

Don't forget to water the plant.

그 식물에 물을 주는 것을 잊지 마.

18 plate
[pleit]

명 접시

His hobby is collecting pretty plates.

그의 취미는 예쁜 접시들을 모으는 것이다.

19 playground
[pléigràund]

명 운동장, 놀이터

Kids are shouting in the playground.

아이들이 놀이터에서 소리치고 있다.

20 plum
[plʌm]

명 자두

Would you like plum jam on the bread?

빵 위에 자두 잼을 발라 줄까요?

Daily Test

A 우리말 뜻과 일치하도록 빠진 글자를 써넣어 단어를 완성하세요.

1 깃발   _ _ _ g   **2** 식물; 심다   _ _ _ _ t

3 자두   _ _ u _   **4** 플루트   _ _ u t _

5 밀가루   _ _ o _ r

B 다음 영어 단어의 우리말 뜻을 쓰세요.

1 flood   __________   **2** plate   __________

3 plan   __________   **4** flower   __________

5 playground   __________

C 우리말 뜻과 일치하도록 빈칸에 알맞은 단어를 써넣어 문장을 완성하세요.

1 Their faces are covered with __________.
그들의 얼굴은 밀가루로 뒤덮여 있다.

2 The bees are looking for a __________.
그 벌들은 꽃을 찾고 있다.

3 Would you like __________ jam on the bread?
빵 위에 자두 잼을 발라 줄까요?

4 The __________ damaged the town.
그 홍수는 그 도시를 훼손했다.

5 Kids are shouting in the __________.
아이들이 놀이터에서 소리치고 있다.

6 Can you raise the __________ higher?
너는 그 깃발을 더 높이 들 수 있니?

7 I __________ to lose weight.
나는 살을 뺄 계획을 세웠다.

8 Bill is playing the __________ in the garden.
Bill은 정원에서 플루트를 연주하고 있다.

01 crab
[kræb]
명 게
A big crab appeared at the beach.
큰 게 한 마리가 해변에 나타났다.

02 crayon
[kréiɑn]
명 크레용
My little sister broke my crayons.
나의 여동생이 나의 크레용들을 부러뜨렸다.

03 cream
[kri:m]
명 크림
Let's mix the cream and the sugar.
그 크림과 그 설탕을 섞자.

04 create
[kriéit]
동 창조하다, 만들다
He created a new hair style.
그는 새로운 헤어 스타일을 만들어 냈다.

05 crowd
[kraud]
명 사람들, 군중, 무리
A crowd gathered around the building.
군중이 그 건물 주위에 모였다.

06 drawer
[drɔ:r]
명 서랍
Dad put the key in the drawer.
아빠는 그 열쇠를 서랍에 넣으셨다.

07 dream
[dri:m]
명 꿈 동 꿈을 꾸다
In my dream, a car was flying in the sky.
나의 꿈 속에서, 자동차가 하늘을 날고 있었다.

08 drive
[draiv]
동 운전하다 ✿ drive-drove-driven
When did you learn to drive?
너는 언제 운전하는 것을 배웠니?

09 drop
[drɑp]
동 떨어지다, 떨어뜨리다
Don't drop the glass bottle.
그 유리병을 떨어뜨리지 마.

10 drum
[drʌm]
명 북, 드럼
She plays the drums in a band.
그녀는 밴드에서 드럼을 친다.

Daily Test

A 우리말 뜻과 일치하도록 빠진 글자를 써넣어 단어를 완성하세요.

1 사람들, 군중, 무리   _ _ _ w _　　**2** 크림   _ _ e _ m

3 운전하다   _ _ _ v _　　**4** 크레용   _ _ a _ o _

5 떨어지다, 떨어뜨리다   _ _ o _

B 다음 영어 단어의 우리말 뜻을 쓰세요.

1 drum   ________________　　**2** create   ________________

3 crab   ________________　　**4** dream   ________________

5 drawer   ________________

C 우리말 뜻과 일치하도록 빈칸에 알맞은 단어를 써넣어 문장을 완성하세요.

1 In my ________________, a car was flying in the sky.
나의 꿈 속에서, 자동차가 하늘을 날고 있었다.

2 A big ________________ appeared at the beach.
큰 게 한 마리가 해변에 나타났다.

3 My little sister broke my ________________.
나의 여동생이 나의 크레용들을 부러뜨렸다.

4 A ________________ gathered around the building.
군중이 그 건물 주위에 모였다.

5 Dad put the key in the ________________.
아빠는 그 열쇠를 서랍에 넣으셨다.

6 When did you learn to ________________?
너는 언제 운전하는 것을 배웠니?

7 Let's mix the ________________ and the sugar.
그 크림과 그 설탕을 섞자.

8 Don't ________________ the glass bottle.
그 유리병을 떨어뜨리지 마.

Day 32 fr-

11 frame
[freim]

명 틀, 액자
I hung the picture frame on the wall.
나는 그 사진틀을 벽에 걸었다.

12 free
[friː]

형 자유로운
Please feel free to eat these sandwiches.
이 샌드위치들을 자유롭게 드세요.

13 freeze
[friːz]

동 얼다, 얼리다 ✿ freeze-froze-frozen
Tomatoes don't freeze well.
토마토는 잘 얼지 않는다.

14 fresh
[freʃ]

형 신선한
He wants fresh milk and bread.
그는 신선한 우유와 빵을 원한다.

15 friend
[frend]

명 친구
I invited my friends to the party.
나는 그 파티에 나의 친구들을 초대했다.

16 frog
[frɔːg]

명 개구리
A tiny frog is sitting on the leaf.
아주 작은 개구리가 나뭇잎 위에 앉아 있다.

17 from
[frəm]

전 ~에서, ~부터
The teenager ran from the park to the bank.
그 십 대는 공원에서 은행까지 달렸다.

18 front
[frʌnt]

명 앞쪽 형 앞쪽의
There is a dog picture on the front of this book.
이 책의 앞면에는 개 그림이 있다.

19 frost
[frɔ(ː)st]

명 서리
There is no frost on the grass.
풀 위에 서리가 없다.

20 fruit
[fruːt]

명 과일
We can make juice with these fruits.
우리는 이 과일들로 주스를 만들 수 있다.

Daily Test

A 우리말 뜻과 일치하도록 빠진 글자를 써넣어 단어를 완성하세요.

1 ~에서, ~부터   __ __ o __

2 개구리   __ __ o __

3 앞쪽; 앞쪽의   __ __ __ n __

4 자유로운   __ __ e __

5 친구   __ __ i __ __ d

B 다음 영어 단어의 우리말 뜻을 쓰세요.

1 fruit _______________

2 fresh _______________

3 frost _______________

4 frame _______________

5 freeze _______________

C 우리말 뜻과 일치하도록 빈칸에 알맞은 단어를 써넣어 문장을 완성하세요.

1 I invited my _______________ to the party.
나는 그 파티에 나의 친구들을 초대했다.

2 He wants _______________ milk and bread.
그는 신선한 우유와 빵을 원한다.

3 There is a dog picture on the _______________ of this book.
이 책의 앞면에는 개 그림이 있다.

4 The teenager ran _______________ the park to the bank.
그 십 대는 공원에서 은행까지 달렸다.

5 There is no _______________ on the grass.
풀 위에 서리가 없다.

6 A tiny _______________ is sitting on the leaf.
아주 작은 개구리가 나뭇잎 위에 앉아 있다.

7 We can make juice with these _______________.
우리는 이 과일들로 주스를 만들 수 있다.

8 I hung the picture _______________ on the wall.
나는 그 사진틀을 벽에 걸었다.

01 skate [skeit]
동 스케이트를 타다
I don't want to skate today.
나는 오늘 스케이트를 타고 싶지 않다.

02 sketch [sketʃ]
명 스케치 동 스케치하다
The artist is sketching with a pencil.
그 화가는 연필로 스케치를 하고 있다.

03 skill [skil]
명 기술, 기량
They need to learn the basic skills.
그들은 그 기본 기술들을 배워야 한다.

04 skin [skin]
명 피부
The baby's skin is soft and clear.
그 아기의 피부는 부드럽고 깨끗하다.

05 skip [skip]
동 깡충깡충 뛰다
Kids were skipping and singing outside.
아이들이 밖에서 깡충깡충 뛰며 노래 부르고 있었다.

06 skirt [skə:rt]
명 치마
That pink skirt is too big for me.
저 분홍색 치마는 나에게 너무 크다.

07 small [smɔːl]
형 작은
I built a small hut in the forest.
나는 숲 속에 작은 오두막을 지었다.

08 smell [smel]
동 ~ 냄새가 나다 명 냄새
This cheese has a bad smell.
이 치즈는 안 좋은 냄새가 난다.

09 smoke [smouk]
명 연기
Smoke is coming out of the chimney.
연기가 굴뚝에서 나오고 있다.

10 smooth [smu:ð]
형 매끄러운, 매끈한
This stone has a smooth surface.
이 돌멩이는 표면이 매끄럽다.

Daily Test

A 우리말 뜻과 일치하도록 빠진 글자를 써넣어 단어를 완성하세요.

1 매끄러운, 매끈한   __ __ o __ t __   2 스케이트를 타다   __ __ a __ e

3 피부   __ __ i __   4 연기   __ __ o k __

5 ~ 냄새가 나다; 냄새   __ __ e __ l

B 다음 영어 단어의 우리말 뜻을 쓰세요.

1 skirt   ________________   2 sketch   ________________

3 skill   ________________   4 skip   ________________

5 small   ________________

C 우리말 뜻과 일치하도록 빈칸에 알맞은 단어를 써넣어 문장을 완성하세요.

1 The artist is ________________ with a pencil.
그 화가는 연필로 스케치를 하고 있다.

2 That pink ________________ is too big for me.
저 분홍색 치마는 나에게 너무 크다.

3 I don't want to ________________ today.
나는 오늘 스케이트를 타고 싶지 않다.

4 ________________ is coming out of the chimney.
연기가 굴뚝에서 나오고 있다.

5 This cheese has a bad ________________.
이 치즈는 안 좋은 냄새가 난다.

6 Kids were ________________ and singing outside.
아이들이 밖에서 깡충깡충 뛰며 노래 부르고 있었다.

7 The baby's ________________ is soft and clear.
그 아기의 피부는 부드럽고 깨끗하다.

8 I built a ________________ hut in the forest.
나는 숲 속에 작은 오두막을 지었다.

11 snail
[sneil]

명 달팽이
Snails move very slowly.
달팽이들은 매우 느리게 움직인다.

12 snake
[sneik]

명 뱀
Some **snakes** have poison.
어떤 뱀들은 독을 가지고 있다.

13 sneakers
[sní:kərz]

명 운동화
He was walking in brown **sneakers**.
그는 갈색 운동화를 신고 걷고 있었다.

14 sneeze
[sni:z]

동 재채기하다
I can't stop **sneezing**.
나는 재채기를 멈출 수가 없다.

15 snow
[snou]

명 눈 동 눈이 오다
White **snow** covered trees and bushes.
하얀 눈이 나무와 덤불을 덮었다.

16 space
[speis]

명 공간
There is a wide **space** in the basement.
지하실에 넓은 공간이 있다.

17 speak
[spi:k]

동 말하다 ✿ speak-spoke-spoken
Please **speak** louder.
더 크게 말해 주세요.

18 speed
[spi:d]

명 속도
The car reduced **speed** and turned right.
그 자동차는 속도를 줄이고 우회전했다.

19 spicy
[spáisi]

형 매운, 맛이 강한
The soup is **spicy** but delicious.
그 수프는 맵지만 맛있다.

20 spider
[spáidər]

명 거미
The **spider** is making a web again.
그 거미는 다시 거미집을 만들고 있다.

Daily Test

A 우리말 뜻과 일치하도록 빠진 글자를 써넣어 단어를 완성하세요.

1 눈; 눈이 오다 　＿ ＿ o ＿　　　2 매운, 맛이 강한 　＿ ＿ ＿ c y

3 달팽이 　＿ ＿ ＿ i ＿　　　4 공간 　＿ ＿ a c ＿

5 운동화 　＿ ＿ e ＿ k ＿ ＿ s

B 다음 영어 단어의 우리말 뜻을 쓰세요.

1 speak 　＿＿＿＿＿＿＿＿＿　　　2 snake 　＿＿＿＿＿＿＿＿＿

3 speed 　＿＿＿＿＿＿＿＿＿　　　4 sneeze 　＿＿＿＿＿＿＿＿＿

5 spider 　＿＿＿＿＿＿＿＿＿

C 우리말 뜻과 일치하도록 빈칸에 알맞은 단어를 써넣어 문장을 완성하세요.

1 White ＿＿＿＿＿＿＿＿＿ covered trees and bushes.
　하얀 눈이 나무와 덤불을 덮었다.

2 The car reduced ＿＿＿＿＿＿＿＿＿ and turned right.
　그 자동차는 속도를 줄이고 우회전했다.

3 The ＿＿＿＿＿＿＿＿＿ is making a web again.
　그 거미는 다시 거미집을 만들고 있다.

4 ＿＿＿＿＿＿＿＿＿ move very slowly.
　달팽이들은 매우 느리게 움직인다.

5 There is a wide ＿＿＿＿＿＿＿＿＿ in the basement.
　지하실에 넓은 공간이 있다.

6 Some ＿＿＿＿＿＿＿＿＿ have poison.
　어떤 뱀들은 독을 가지고 있다.

7 Please ＿＿＿＿＿＿＿＿＿ louder.
　더 크게 말해 주세요.

8 He was walking in brown ＿＿＿＿＿＿＿＿＿.
　그는 갈색 운동화를 신고 걷고 있었다.

| 01 | **knee** [niː] | 몡 무릎
It is going to protect my knee**s**.
그것은 나의 무릎을 보호해 줄 것이다. |

01 knee [niː]
몡 무릎
It is going to protect my knees.
그것은 나의 무릎을 보호해 줄 것이다.

02 knife [naif]
몡 칼
I need a knife to cut the cake.
나는 그 케이크를 자르기 위해 칼이 필요하다.

03 knight [nait]
몡 기사
The boy drew a prince and a knight.
그 소년은 왕자와 기사를 그렸다.

04 knit [nit]
통 뜨다, 뜨개질을 하다
Did he knit the hat by himself?
그는 그 모자를 직접 떴니?

05 knock [nɑk]
통 두드리다, 노크하다
The woman knocked and entered the room.
그 여자는 노크하고 그 방에 들어갔다.

06 know [nou]
통 알다, 알고 있다　✿ know-knew-known
Do you know who he is?
너는 그가 누구인지 아니?

07 design [dizáin]
몡 디자인　통 설계하다
My client wants to change the design.
나의 고객은 그 디자인을 바꾸고 싶어 한다.

08 foreign [fɔ́ːrin]
형 외국의
Can she speak any foreign languages?
그녀는 외국어를 말할 수 있니?

09 resign [rizáin]
통 사임하다
The mayor decided to resign.
그 시장은 사임하기로 결정했다.

10 sign [sain]
몡 표지판　통 서명하다
Sign on the back of the card.
그 카드 뒷면에 서명해.

Daily Test

A 우리말 뜻과 일치하도록 빠진 글자를 써넣어 단어를 완성하세요.

1 두드리다, 노크하다   __ __ o c __

2 표지판; 서명하다   __ __ g __

3 뜨다, 뜨개질을 하다   __ __ __ t

4 알다, 알고 있다   __ n __ __

5 무릎   __ __ e __

B 다음 영어 단어의 우리말 뜻을 쓰세요.

1 knight   ________________

2 resign   ________________

3 design   ________________

4 knife   ________________

5 foreign   ________________

C 우리말 뜻과 일치하도록 빈칸에 알맞은 단어를 써넣어 문장을 완성하세요.

1 The woman ________________ and entered the room.
그 여자는 노크하고 그 방에 들어갔다.

2 The mayor decided to ________________.
그 시장은 사임하기로 결정했다.

3 The boy drew a prince and a ________________.
그 소년은 왕자와 기사를 그렸다.

4 My client wants to change the ________________.
나의 고객은 그 디자인을 바꾸고 싶어 한다.

5 I need a ________________ to cut the cake.
나는 그 케이크를 자르기 위해 칼이 필요하다.

6 ________________ on the back of the card.
그 카드 뒷면에 서명해.

7 Do you ________________ who he is?
너는 그가 누구인지 아니?

8 Did he ________________ the hat by himself?
그는 그 모자를 직접 떴니?

11 bomb
[bɑm]

명 폭탄
The police officer found a bomb.
그 경찰관은 폭탄을 발견했다.

12 climb
[klaim]

동 오르다, 올라가다
It was foggy, but I climbed the mountain.
안개가 꼈지만, 나는 산에 올라갔다.

13 comb
[koum]

명 빗
Will you return my comb?
나의 빗을 돌려 줄래?

14 lamb
[læm]

명 새끼 양
The farmer is watching the lamb.
그 농부는 그 새끼 양을 지켜보고 있다.

15 thumb
[θʌm]

명 엄지손가락
The cat scratched his thumb.
그 고양이는 그의 엄지손가락을 할퀴었다.

16 wrap
[ræp]

동 싸다, 포장하다
We must wrap these goods today.
우리는 오늘 이 상품들을 포장해야 한다.

17 wrinkle
[ríŋkl]

명 주름
Wrinkles around his eyes are charming.
그의 눈가에 있는 주름은 매력적이다.

18 wrist
[rist]

명 손목, 팔목
Mom is wearing a watch on her wrist.
엄마는 손목에 손목시계를 차고 계시다.

19 write
[rait]

동 쓰다 ✿ write-wrote-written
She was writing her address on the letter.
그녀는 편지에 그녀의 주소를 쓰고 있었다.

20 wrong
[rɔ(ː)ŋ]

형 틀린, 잘못된
I put an X on the wrong answer.
나는 틀린 답 위에 X표를 했다.

Daily Test

A 우리말 뜻과 일치하도록 빠진 글자를 써넣어 단어를 완성하세요.

1 오르다, 올라가다   __ l __ __ __

2 빗   __ o __ __

3 틀린, 잘못된   __ __ o __ g

4 싸다, 포장하다   __ __ __ p

5 주름   __ __ __ n k __ __

B 다음 영어 단어의 우리말 뜻을 쓰세요.

1 write   ________________

2 bomb   ________________

3 thumb   ________________

4 wrist   ________________

5 lamb   ________________

C 우리말 뜻과 일치하도록 빈칸에 알맞은 단어를 써넣어 문장을 완성하세요.

1 It was foggy, but I ________________ the mountain.
안개가 꼈지만, 나는 산에 올라갔다.

2 We must ________________ these goods today.
우리는 오늘 이 상품들을 포장해야 한다.

3 She was ________________ her address on the letter.
그녀는 편지에 그녀의 주소를 쓰고 있었다.

4 Will you return my ________________?
나의 빗을 돌려 줄래?

5 Mom is wearing a watch on her ________________.
엄마는 손목에 손목시계를 차고 계시다.

6 The police officer found a ________________.
그 경찰관은 폭탄을 발견했다.

7 The cat scratched his ________________.
그 고양이는 그의 엄지손가락을 할퀴었다.

8 The farmer is watching the ________________.
그 농부는 그 새끼 양을 지켜보고 있다.

A 우리말 뜻에 해당하는 영어 단어를 찾아 동그라미 하세요.

| 칼 | 피부 | 불다 | 자두 | 얼다, 얼리다 |
| 점원 | 크림 | 운전하다 | 달팽이 | 오르다, 올라가다 |

s	p	f	r	e	e	z	e	c	w
k	v	g	d	l	g	s	p	l	l
i	c	l	i	m	b	r	t	e	h
n	c	a	w	m	l	h	z	r	k
t	n	j	a	h	o	t	d	k	n
s	b	e	l	k	w	k	g	w	i
d	r	b	f	d	r	i	v	e	f
c	h	p	l	u	m	w	b	t	e

B 우리말 뜻과 일치하도록 알맞은 단어를 골라 문장을 완성하세요.

| plates | skills | clapping | free | wrinkles | spicy |

1 The soup is _______________ but delicious.
그 수프는 맵지만 맛있다.

2 _______________ is a way to show respect.
박수를 치는 것은 존경심을 나타내는 방법이다.

3 His hobby is collecting pretty _______________.
그의 취미는 예쁜 접시들을 모으는 것이다.

4 Please feel _______________ to eat these sandwiches.
이 샌드위치들을 자유롭게 드세요.

5 _______________ around his eyes are charming.
그의 눈가에 있는 주름은 매력적이다.

6 They need to learn the basic _______________.
그들은 그 기본 기술들을 배워야 한다.

Day 35

Day 35_C

C 들려 주는 영어 단어를 바르게 쓴 다음, 우리말 뜻을 써넣으세요.

	영어 단어	우리말		영어 단어	우리말
1			11		
2			12		
3			13		
4			14		
5			15		
6			16		
7			17		
8			18		
9			19		
10			20		

D 우리말 뜻과 일치하도록 알맞은 단어를 골라 동그라미 하세요.

1 I can't stop (sneezing / speaking).
나는 재채기를 멈출 수가 없다.

2 The peach (black / blossom) smells sweet.
그 복숭아꽃은 달콤한 냄새가 난다.

3 There is a dog picture on the (frog / front) of this book.
이 책의 앞면에는 개 그림이 있다.

4 She plays the (dreams / drums) in a band.
그녀는 밴드에서 드럼을 친다.

5 Can she speak any (foreign / design) languages?
그녀는 외국어를 말할 수 있니?

6 I put an X on the (wrong / wrist) answer.
나는 틀린 답 위에 X표를 했다.

1	block	______________	2	꿈; 꿈을 꾸다 ______________
3	sketch	______________	4	거미 ______________
5	knock	______________	6	친구 ______________
7	small	______________	8	말하다 ______________
9	crayon	______________	10	사임하다 ______________
11	bomb	______________	12	밀가루 ______________
13	flower	______________	14	틀, 액자 ______________
15	wrist	______________	16	과일 ______________
17	snake	______________	18	새끼 양 ______________
19	clean	______________	20	운동장, 놀이터 ______________

Day 35_F

1 Don't forget to water the ______________.

2 There is no ______________ on the grass.

3 White ______________ covered trees and bushes.

4 It is going to protect my ______________.

5 This stone has a ______________ surface.

6 She was ______________ her address on the letter.

7 The ______________ man is walking with a guide dog.

8 He ______________ a new hair style.

G 우리말 뜻과 일치하도록 빈칸에 알맞은 단어를 써넣어 문장을 완성하세요.

1 The boy drew a prince and a k________________.
그 소년은 왕자와 기사를 그렸다.

2 The cat scratched his t________________.
그 고양이는 그의 엄지손가락을 할퀴었다.

3 She attends the guitar c________________ after work.
그녀는 퇴근 후에 기타 동호회에 참석한다.

4 The teenager ran f________________ the park to the bank.
그 십 대는 공원에서 은행까지 달렸다.

5 Dad put the key in the d________________.
아빠는 그 열쇠를 서랍에 넣으셨다.

6 Bill is playing the f________________ in the garden.
Bill은 정원에서 플루트를 연주하고 있다.

7 There is a wide s________________ in the basement.
지하실에 넓은 공간이 있다.

8 S________________ is coming out of the chimney.
연기가 굴뚝에서 나오고 있다.

9 That pink s________________ is too big for me.
저 분홍색 치마는 나에게 너무 크다.

10 My client wants to change the d________________.
나의 고객은 그 디자인을 바꾸고 싶어 한다.

✎ Review에서 틀린 문제의 영어 단어와 우리말 뜻을 쓴 다음, 영어 단어를 3번씩 쓰세요.

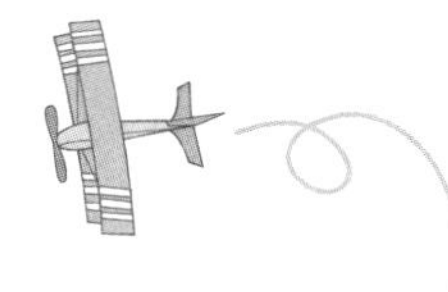

Answer Key

Answer Key

Day 01
p. 8

A 1 hamburger 2 beef 3 pepper
4 curry 5 chocolate

B 1 생선, 물고기 2 국수 3 닭고기, 닭
4 아이스크림 5 커피

C 1 chicken 2 Ice cream 3 chocolate
4 Fish 5 beef 6 curry 7 pepper
8 coffee

Day 01
p. 10

A 1 sauce 2 salad 3 sugar 4 pork
5 sausage

B 1 쌀, 밥, 벼 2 스파게티 3 소금 4 탄산음료
5 샌드위치

C 1 salad 2 sausage 3 sandwiches
4 soda 5 salt 6 spaghetti 7 sauce
8 rice

Day 02
p. 12

A 1 rabbit 2 koala 3 dolphin 4 branch
5 seal

B 1 악어 2 거위 3 꽃; 꽃을 피우다 4 쥐
5 꽃봉오리, 싹

C 1 rabbit 2 alligators 3 koala 4 branch
5 blossom 6 mouse 7 seal 8 goose

Day 02
p. 14

A 1 trunk 2 whale 3 sheep 4 turtle
5 seed

B 1 줄기 2 거미 3 다람쥐 4 잡초
5 나무, 목재

C 1 stem 2 spider 3 wood 4 sheep
5 turtle 6 seeds 7 squirrel 8 whale

Day 03
p. 16

A 1 picnic 2 camping 3 cancel
4 fireworks 5 hiking

B 1 휴일, 휴가 2 해외로, 해외에 3 시골 지역
4 짐, 수하물 5 호텔

C 1 countryside 2 picnic 3 hiking
4 baggage 5 camping 6 hotel
7 cancel 8 holiday

Day 03
p. 18

A 1 trip 2 sunglasses 3 tent 4 swimsuit
5 plan

B 1 여행하다 2 관광 3 관광객 4 방학, 휴가
5 수영장

C 1 tent 2 pool 3 tourists 4 vacation
5 trip 6 plan 7 travels 8 swimsuit

Day 04
p. 20

A 1 cart 2 coin 3 cheap 4 cash
5 customer

B 1 점원 2 신용 카드 3 사다
4 값, 비용; (값이) ~이다 5 할인; 할인하다

C 1 buys 2 customer 3 Carts
4 credit card 5 cash 6 coins
7 cheap 8 clerk

p. 22

A 1 grocery 2 save 3 shop 4 pay
5 dollar

B 1 비싼 2 진열하다; 전시, 진열 3 낭비하다; 낭비
4 환불; 환불하다 5 영수증

C 1 pay 2 display 3 waste 4 shop
5 grocery 6 saving 7 expensive
8 refund

p. 23

A

g	p	w	c	p	j	s	k	l	p
b	e	e	f	i	m	a	z	q	r
d	s	e	m	c	h	l	m	n	t
g	w	d	l	n	s	t	e	m	r
c	o	i	n	i	h	h	t	j	a
q	y	o	b	c	o	j	v	d	v
n	g	t	s	h	p	k	o	z	e
v	f	x	r	e	c	s	t	m	l

B 1 plan 2 hamburgers 3 expensive
4 cost 5 buds 6 holiday

C

	영어 단어	우리말
1	branch	나뭇가지
2	camping	캠핑, 야영
3	display	진열하다; 전시, 진열
4	fish	생선, 물고기
5	trip	여행
6	sausage	소시지
7	pool	수영장
8	spider	거미
9	alligator	악어
10	pepper	후추
11	credit card	신용 카드
12	salad	샐러드
13	save	저축하다, 절약하다
14	fireworks	불꽃놀이
15	rabbit	토끼
16	cart	카트, 수레
17	noodles	국수
18	dollar	달러
19	tent	텐트, 천막
20	whale	고래

D 1 chicken 2 baggage 3 mouse
4 sauce 5 cheap 6 seeds

E 1 현금 2 spaghetti 3 할인; 할인하다
4 cancel 5 거북 6 ice cream 7 샌드위치
8 sightseeing 9 나무, 목재 10 pay
11 코알라 12 vacation 13 관광객
14 blossom 15 낭비하다; 낭비 16 sheep
17 하이킹, 도보 여행 18 coffee 19 쌀, 밥, 벼
20 clerk

F 1 seal 2 curry 3 abroad 4 trunk
5 customer 6 pork 7 swimsuit
8 grocery

G 1 buys 2 chocolate 3 countryside
4 sunglasses 5 dolphin 6 receipt
7 sugar 8 hotel 9 squirrel 10 refund

p. 28

A 1 bakery 2 farm 3 harbor
4 aquarium 5 church

B 1 은행 2 소방서 3 공항 4 서점 5 약국

C 1 church 2 harbor 3 bank 4 aquarium
5 bookstore 6 fire station 7 drugstore
8 bakery

Day 10

p. 43

A

z	v	w	v	h	j	m	q	p	g
f	a	i	r	z	a	o	d	s	r
l	h	h	v	l	l	r	i	v	e
y	b	p	n	a	o	b	b	n	e
b	q	c	d	n	n	f	w	o	t
a	g	r	a	d	e	x	g	v	r
n	h	w	s	t	u	d	y	f	g
k	t	k	j	m	C	h	i	n	a

B 1 attend 2 favor 3 national 4 theaters
5 Europe 6 farm

C

	영어 단어	우리말
1	hug	껴안다
2	bakery	빵집, 제과점
3	gym	체육관
4	post office	우체국
5	timetable	시간표
6	Australia	호주
7	fire station	소방서
8	bow	(고개 숙여) 인사하다
9	Russia	러시아
10	cafeteria	구내 식당, 카페테리아
11	America	미국, 아메리카 대륙
12	club	클럽, 동호회
13	thank	고마워하다
14	church	교회
15	England	영국
16	apology	사과
17	music room	음악실
18	friend	친구
19	park	공원
20	Japan	일본

D 1 exam 2 appointment 3 uniforms
4 airport 5 partner 6 ocean

E 1 도와주다; 도움 2 Africa 3 익숙한, 친숙한
4 restaurant 5 미술실 6 introduce
7 아시아 8 classroom 9 약국
10 playground 11 프랑스 12 school
13 도서관 14 Korea 15 행동
16 graduate 17 병원 18 Canada
19 스페인 20 police station

F 1 classmate 2 fault 3 country
4 bookstore 5 Italy 6 museum
7 semester 8 refused

G 1 market 2 principal 3 admire
4 shares 5 aquarium 6 continents
7 absent 8 stadium 9 friendship
10 region

Day 11

p. 48

A 1 third 2 first 3 ninth 4 fifth
5 eighth

B 1 여섯 번째의, 제6의 2 열 번째의, 제10의
3 두 번째의, 제2의 4 네 번째의, 제4의
5 일곱 번째의, 제7의

C 1 first 2 eighth 3 seventh 4 fourth
5 second 6 ninth 7 sixth 8 fifth

Day 11

p. 50

A 1 twelfth 2 twentieth 3 sixteenth
4 eleventh 5 fourteenth

B 1 열일곱 번째의, 제17의 2 열세 번째의, 제13의
3 열아홉 번째의, 제19의 4 열다섯 번째의, 제15의
5 열여덟 번째의, 제18의

C 1 sixteenth 2 seventeenth 3 thirteenth
4 twelfth 5 eleventh 6 nineteenth
7 fifteenth 8 fourteenth

Day 12

p. 52

A 1 castle 2 entrance 3 bridge 4 aisle
5 building

B 1 엘리베이터 2 지하층, 지하실
3 짓다, 건설하다 4 천장 5 울타리

C 1 entrance 2 castle 3 basement
4 elevator 5 fence 6 building
7 bridge 8 ceiling

Day 12

p. 54

A 1 garage 2 wall 3 tower 4 hall
5 pyramid

B 1 구조, 구조물 2 오두막 3 계단 4 지붕
5 절, 사원

C 1 garage 2 structure 3 hut 4 wall
5 temple 6 roof 7 pyramid 8 tower

Day 13

p. 56

A 1 grow 2 born 3 cook 4 adopt
5 birth

B 1 돌봄, 보살핌 2 고치다 3 설거지
4 (일상적인) 일 5 먹이를 주다

C 1 grew 2 adopt 3 dishwashing
4 cooks 5 feed 6 fix 7 born
8 chores

Day 13

p. 58

A 1 lawn 2 marry 3 pregnant 4 raise
5 laundry

B 1 사랑; 사랑하다 2 집 3 가정
4 결혼 생활, 결혼 5 다리미질

C 1 marry 2 laundry 3 household
4 ironing 5 lawn 6 raise 7 loves
8 home

Day 14

p. 60

A 1 donate 2 group 3 main 4 gather
5 learn

B 1 사업, 업무 2 사람들, 군중, 무리 3 부족, 결핍
4 지역 사회, 지역 주민 5 변하다, 바꾸다; 변화

C 1 donate 2 main 3 crowd 4 lack
5 changed 6 groups 7 business
8 gathered

Day 14

p. 62

A 1 pass 2 speak 3 role 4 think
5 print

B 1 쓰다 2 구성원, 회원 3 약속하다
4 질문, 문제 5 발표

C 1 role 2 promised 3 members 4 pass
5 presentation 6 write 7 thinking
8 print

Day 15

p. 63

A

c	r	c	z	s	t	l	a	c	k
y	b	o	r	n	b	n	o	z	t
c	b	o	b	p	x	r	k	v	w
a	v	k	g	v	x	c	f	c	e
s	i	x	t	h	h	o	d	v	l
t	j	s	k	f	o	h	r	k	f
l	f	g	p	r	i	n	t	g	t
e	q	c	r	o	w	d	k	h	h

B 1 stairs 2 community 3 eighteenth

4 build 5 care 6 tenth

C

	영어 단어	우리말
1	second	두 번째의, 제2의
2	basement	지하층, 지하실
3	pyramid	피라미드
4	ironing	다리미질
5	seventeenth	열일곱 번째의, 제17의
6	donate	기부하다
7	fence	울타리
8	chore	(일상적인) 일
9	eighth	여덟 번째의, 제8의
10	presentation	발표
11	grow	자라다
12	fourteenth	열네 번째의, 제14의
13	main	주된
14	building	건물
15	wall	벽, 담
16	fifth	다섯 번째의, 제5의
17	raise	키우다
18	role	역할
19	garage	차고, 주차장
20	write	쓰다

D 1 birth 2 hall 3 learn 4 questions
5 twentieth 6 marriage

E 1 네 번째의, 제4의 2 nineteenth 3 약속하다
4 hut 5 절, 사원 6 elevator
7 (~와) 결혼하다 8 think 9 집
10 seventh 11 다리 12 member
13 변하다, 바꾸다; 변화 14 laundry
15 열세 번째의, 제13의 16 fix
17 모이다, 모으다 18 adopt 19 입구, 문
20 fifteenth

F 1 feed 2 first 3 ceiling 4 groups
5 tower 6 sixteenth 7 pass 8 lawn

G 1 speak 2 aisle 3 dishwashing 4 ninth
5 eleventh 6 pregnant 7 business
8 household 9 Third 10 structure

Day 16

p. 68

A 1 bean 2 crab 3 melon 4 kiwi
5 cucumber

B 1 자두 2 견과 3 생강 4 브로콜리 5 상추

C 1 plums 2 kiwi 3 beans 4 melons
5 broccoli 6 lettuce 7 Ginger 8 crabs

Day 16

p. 70

A 1 squid 2 tomato 3 seafood 4 shrimp
5 strawberry

B 1 시금치 2 조개류 3 호박 4 수박
5 고구마

C 1 shrimps 2 Strawberry 3 tomatoes
4 Squids 5 shellfish 6 sweet potatoes
7 watermelon 8 spinach

Day 17

p. 72

A 1 fever 2 cancer 3 die 4 dizzy
5 cough

B 1 질병 2 감기 3 두통 4 식단, 다이어트
5 죽음

C 1 headache 2 death 3 cancer
4 cough 5 disease 6 cold 7 fever
8 died

Day 17

p. 74

A 1 patient 2 hurt 3 sick 4 heal

5 medicine

B 1 위통, 복통 2 건강 3 창백한, 핼쑥한
4 재치기하다 5 알약, 정제

C 1 heal 2 sick 3 pale 4 stomachache
5 hurt 6 sneeze 7 patient 8 health

Day 18
p. 76

A 1 answer 2 computer 3 call 4 agree
5 announce

B 1 담소를 나누다; 담소 2 의사소통을 하다
3 동의하지 않다 4 묻다, 물어 보다 5 설명하다

C 1 explained 2 answer 3 Computers
4 announce 5 disagree 6 Ask
7 communicate 8 call

Day 18
p. 78

A 1 letter 2 fact 3 humor 4 news
5 Internet

B 1 우편, 우편물 2 농담 3 몸짓, 제스처
4 (공식적으로) 알리다 5 전화기

C 1 Internet 2 gesture 3 phone 4 news
5 letter 6 facts 7 joke 8 mail

Day 19
p. 80

A 1 before 2 forever 3 early 4 dawn
5 afternoon

B 1 저녁 2 (얼마의 시간) 전에 3 끝, 종료
4 ~ 동안, ~ 내내 5 ~ 뒤에, ~ 후에

C 1 during 2 after 3 before 4 afternoon
5 early 6 evening 7 ago 8 forever

Day 19
p. 82

A 1 morning 2 noon 3 night 4 next
5 present

B 1 자정, 밤 12시 2 과거; 지난, 이전의
3 미래; 미래의 4 지난, 마지막의 5 늦은; 늦게

C 1 midnight 2 future 3 past 4 last
5 noon 6 morning 7 night 8 present

Day 20
p. 83

A

m	z	k	i	w	i	j	n	y	h
a	c	q	s	d	t	p	g	h	p
i	r	t	b	s	y	c	h	e	r
l	a	s	a	d	k	t	a	a	c
c	b	l	x	n	o	o	n	l	o
e	a	r	l	y	h	j	k	j	l
x	t	m	g	x	s	y	w	l	d
j	s	q	u	i	d	p	z	h	n

B 1 next 2 pumpkins 3 humor 4 pill
5 chat 6 dizzy

C

	영어 단어	우리말
1	cough	기침하다; 기침
2	joke	농담
3	bean	콩
4	health	건강
5	afternoon	오후
6	communicate	의사소통을 하다
7	during	~ 동안, ~ 내내
8	plum	자두
9	future	미래; 미래의
10	sneeze	재채기하다
11	tomato	토마토
12	answer	대답; 대답하다

13	fever	열
14	news	소식, 뉴스
15	before	~ 전에, ~ 앞에
16	lettuce	상추
17	patient	환자
18	fact	사실
19	night	밤
20	strawberry	딸기

D 1 late 2 agree 3 cancer 4 seafood
5 after 6 cucumbers

E 1 묻다, 물어 보다 2 dawn 3 죽다
4 broccoli 5 몸짓, 제스처 6 past
7 다치게 하다, 아프다 8 headache
9 (얼마의 시간) 전에 10 melon 11 영원히
12 disagree 13 전화기 14 watermelon
15 자정, 밤 12시 16 spinach 17 아픈, 병든
18 stomachache 19 고구마 20 letter

F 1 end 2 present 3 medicine 4 diet
5 shrimps 6 nuts 7 Inform
8 Computers

G 1 announce 2 morning 3 Ginger
4 pale 5 Internet 6 shellfish
7 evening 8 death 9 disease
10 explained

Day 21
p. 88

A 1 deep 2 huge 3 height 4 gram
5 half

B 1 높은; 높이 2 (단위) 킬로그램 3 넓은
4 비교하다 5 거대한

C 1 broad 2 kilograms 3 compared
4 half 5 deep 6 high 7 grams
8 height

Day 21
p. 90

A 1 long 2 small 3 wide 4 large
5 meter

B 1 규모, 범위 2 (단위) 킬로미터 3 매우 작은
4 좁은 5 크기

C 1 narrow 2 scale 3 meters 4 long
5 wide 6 tiny 7 kilometers 8 small

Day 22
p. 92

A 1 danger 2 alive 3 accident 4 escape
5 careful

B 1 귀가 먹은, 청각 장애가 있는
2 눈이 먼, 시각 장애가 있는
3 손상, 피해; 훼손하다 4 비상 (사태) 5 구급차

C 1 damage 2 escaped 3 ambulance
4 blind 5 danger 6 Deaf 7 alive
8 accident

Day 22
p. 94

A 1 safe 2 harm 3 save 4 pain
5 survive

B 1 막다, 예방하다 2 발생하다, 일어나다
3 차량들, 교통(량) 4 부상을 입은, 다친 5 안전

C 1 prevent 2 happen 3 pain
4 survived 5 harm 6 safety
7 saved 8 injured

Day 23
p. 96

A 1 date 2 summer 3 Monday 4 season
5 Saturday

B 1 하루, 날, 요일 2 가을 3 봄 4 생일

5 금요일

C 1 seasons 2 fall 3 spring 4 Monday
5 Friday 6 birthday 7 summer
8 Saturday

Day 23

p. 98

A 1 winter 2 Thursday 3 today
4 Tuesday 5 yesterday

B 1 내일 2 수요일 3 주말 4 일요일
5 주, 일주일

C 1 today 2 Wednesday 3 Thursday
4 Tuesday 5 weekend 6 Sunday
7 yesterday 8 winter

Day 24

p. 100

A 1 freeze 2 dust 3 heat 4 flood
5 lightning

B 1 지진 2 예측; 예측하다 3 얼음 4 허리케인
5 불, 화재

C 1 flood 2 hurricane 3 earthquake
4 dust 5 ice 6 fire 7 Lightning
8 freezes

Day 24

p. 102

A 1 thunder 2 shower 3 melt 4 volcano
5 sunlight

B 1 자연 2 날씨 3 온도, 기온 4 태풍
5 무지개

C 1 thunder 2 temperature 3 weather
4 typhoon 5 rainbow 6 melt
7 shower 8 sunlight

Day 25

p. 103

A

z	x	m	e	l	t	s	h	z	j
f	s	w	r	t	o	l	a	j	s
i	u	t	n	p	d	m	g	v	d
r	m	r	c	w	a	h	g	q	e
e	m	d	t	r	y	g	q	y	p
t	e	p	g	k	w	s	z	d	a
n	r	g	s	m	a	l	l	p	i
a	l	i	v	e	l	o	n	g	n

B 1 forecast 2 emergency 3 giant
4 tomorrow 5 nature 6 days

C

	영어 단어	우리말
1	fall	가을
2	broad	넓은
3	weather	날씨
4	scale	규모, 범위
5	rainbow	무지개
6	blind	눈이 먼, 시각 장애가 있는
7	Wednesday	수요일
8	high	높은; 높이
9	freeze	얼다, 얼리다
10	injured	부상을 입은, 다친
11	accident	사고
12	Thursday	목요일
13	survive	살아남다, 생존하다
14	deep	깊은
15	yesterday	어제
16	season	계절
17	danger	위험
18	temperature	온도, 기온
19	meter	(단위) 미터
20	ice	얼음

D 1 size 2 safe 3 volcano 4 huge
5 careful 6 spring

E 1 발생하다, 일어나다 2 ambulance 3 화요일
4 kilometer 5 비교하다 6 Sunday 7 먼지
8 safety 9 귀가 먹은, 청각 장애가 있는
10 hurricane 11 번개, 번갯불 12 birthday
13 해, 피해; 해치다 14 half 15 좁은
16 weekend 17 소나기 18 tiny
19 월요일 20 thunder

F 1 typhoon 2 wide 3 winter 4 prevent
5 Friday 6 flood 7 damage
8 kilograms

G 1 earthquake 2 large 3 Saturday
4 traffic 5 heat 6 week 7 height
8 escaped 9 date 10 sunlight

Day 26
p. 108

A 1 clever 2 brave 3 kind 4 curious
5 active

B 1 자신감 있는 2 정직한, 솔직한 3 온화한, 순한
4 발랄한, 쾌활한 5 용기

C 1 kind 2 clever 3 cheerful 4 brave
5 confident 6 active 7 curious
8 courage

Day 26
p. 110

A 1 quiet 2 silly 3 passion 4 wise
5 lazy

B 1 똑똑한, 영리한 2 못된, 심술궂은 3 이기적인
4 수다스러운 5 온화한, 순한

C 1 lazy 2 quiet 3 mean 4 mild
5 silly 6 talkative 7 selfish 8 passion

Day 27
p. 112

A 1 author 2 chef 3 athlete 4 dentist
5 announcer

B 1 형사 2 목수 3 건축가 4 경호원, 보디가드
5 우주 비행사

C 1 Astronauts 2 carpenter 3 detective
4 architect 5 chef 6 athlete
7 announcer 8 author

Day 27
p. 114

A 1 lawyer 2 waiter 3 soldier 4 judge
5 sailor

B 1 경찰관 2 동물원 사육사 3 시인
4 엔지니어, 기술자 5 소방관

C 1 judge 2 lawyer 3 waiter 4 engineer
5 zookeeper 6 poet 7 firefighters
8 sailors

Day 28
p. 116

A 1 bald 2 cheek 3 eyebrow 4 beard
5 charming

B 1 겉모습, 외모 2 아름다운 3 보조개
4 우아한 5 이마

C 1 charming 2 elegant 3 forehead
4 beard 5 appearance 6 bald
7 beautiful 8 cheek

Day 28
p. 118

A 1 gum 2 stout 3 gorgeous 4 jaw
5 wonderful

B 1 입술 2 혀 3 콧수염 4 잘생긴

5 과체중의, 비만의

C 1 jaw 2 good-looking 3 overweight
4 wonderful 5 tongue 6 stout
7 mustache 8 gorgeous

Day 29
p. 120

A 1 goods 2 advice 3 duty 4 client
5 file

B 1 도움이 되는 2 지원하다 3 상사 4 회사
5 서식

C 1 boss 2 goods 3 advice 4 client
5 file 6 company 7 apply 8 helpful

Day 29
p. 122

A 1 hire 2 income 3 offer 4 office
5 teamwork

B 1 기획, 프로젝트 2 산업 3 알; 일하다
4 이력서 5 급여, 봉급

C 1 teamwork 2 hired 3 resume
4 project 5 offer 6 work 7 salary
8 office

Day 30
p. 123

A

s	p	t	f	i	l	e	g	z	y
n	t	g	b	p	z	d	q	s	r
c	b	o	s	s	v	w	o	r	k
p	h	c	u	y	r	a	v	z	m
b	p	e	g	t	s	i	l	l	y
a	l	k	f	h	y	t	t	f	r
l	a	z	y	c	l	e	v	e	r
d	p	f	f	d	p	r	g	v	y

B 1 honest 2 soldiers 3 dimples
4 form 5 wisest 6 income

C

	영어 단어	우리말
1	architect	건축가
2	jaw	턱
3	helpful	도움이 되는
4	zookeeper	동물원 사육사
5	active	활동적인, 활발한
6	apply	지원하다
7	engineer	엔지니어, 기술자
8	kind	친절한, 다정한
9	resume	이력서
10	elegant	우아한
11	good-looking	잘생긴
12	mean	못된, 심술궂은
13	author	작가, 저자
14	tongue	혀
15	beautiful	아름다운
16	selfish	이기적인
17	salary	급여, 봉급
18	office	근무처, 사무실
19	confident	자신감 있는
20	poet	시인

D 1 smart 2 dentist 3 lips 4 duties
5 bodyguard 6 eyebrows

E 1 아나운서 2 forehead 3 아주 멋진
4 quiet 5 용감한 6 sailor 7 (턱)수염
8 wonderful 9 기획, 프로젝트 10 athlete
11 발랄한, 쾌활한 12 hire 13 팀워크
14 firefighter 15 과체중의, 비만의
16 client 17 상품, 제품 18 carpenter
19 온화한, 순한 20 cheek

F 1 courage 2 industry 3 detective
4 gums 5 advice 6 lawyer 7 talkative

8 charming

G 1 passion 2 appearance 3 company
4 gentle 5 judge 6 Astronauts 7 offer
8 curious 9 Police officers 10 mustache

Day 31
p. 130

A 1 black 2 club 3 clap 4 block
5 classroom

B 1 꽃; 꽃을 피우다 2 닦다, 청소하다; 깨끗한
3 눈이 먼, 시각 장애가 있는 4 불다 5 점원

C 1 blowing 2 club 3 black 4 classroom
5 blind 6 clerk 7 blocking 8 clean

Day 31
p. 132

A 1 flag 2 plant 3 plum 4 flute 5 flour

B 1 홍수 2 접시 3 계획; 계획을 세우다 4 꽃
5 운동장, 놀이터

C 1 flour 2 flower 3 plum 4 flood
5 playground 6 flag 7 planned 8 flute

Day 32
p. 134

A 1 crowd 2 cream 3 drive 4 crayon
5 drop

B 1 북, 드럼 2 창조하다, 만들다 3 게
4 꿈; 꿈을 꾸다 5 서랍

C 1 dream 2 crab 3 crayons 4 crowd
5 drawer 6 drive 7 cream 8 drop

Day 32
p. 136

A 1 from 2 frog 3 front 4 free 5 friend

B 1 과일 2 신선한 3 서리 4 틀, 액자
5 얼다, 얼리다

C 1 friends 2 fresh 3 front 4 from
5 frost 6 frog 7 fruits 8 frame

Day 33
p. 138

A 1 smooth 2 skate 3 skin 4 smoke
5 smell

B 1 치마 2 스케치; 스케치하다 3 기술, 기량
4 깡충깡충 뛰다 5 작은

C 1 sketching 2 skirt 3 skate 4 Smoke
5 smell 6 skipping 7 skin 8 small

Day 33
p. 140

A 1 snow 2 spicy 3 snail 4 space
5 sneakers

B 1 말하다 2 뱀 3 속도 4 재채기하다
5 거미

C 1 snow 2 speed 3 spider 4 Snails
5 space 6 snakes 7 speak 8 sneakers

Day 34
p. 142

A 1 knock 2 sign 3 knit 4 know
5 knee

B 1 기사 2 사임하다 3 디자인; 설계하다 4 칼
5 외국의

C 1 knocked 2 resign 3 knight 4 design
5 knife 6 Sign 7 know 8 knit

Day 34
p. 144

A 1 climb 2 comb 3 wrong 4 wrap

5 wrinkle

B 1 쓰다 2 폭탄 3 엄지손가락 4 손목, 팔목
5 새끼 양

C 1 climbed 2 wrap 3 writing 4 comb
5 wrist 6 bomb 7 thumb 8 lamb

Day 35

p. 145

A

s	p	f	r	e	e	z	e	c	w
k	v	g	d	l	g	s	p	l	l
i	c	l	i	m	b	r	t	e	h
n	c	a	w	m	l	h	z	r	k
t	n	j	a	h	o	t	d	k	n
s	b	e	l	k	w	k	g	w	i
d	r	b	f	d	r	i	v	e	f
c	h	p	l	u	m	w	b	t	e

B 1 spicy 2 Clapping 3 plates 4 free
5 Wrinkles 6 skills

C

	영어 단어	우리말
1	smell	~ 냄새가 나다; 냄새
2	flag	깃발
3	wrap	싸다, 포장하다
4	crowd	사람들, 군중, 무리
5	speed	속도
6	fresh	신선한
7	plan	계획; 계획을 세우다
8	know	알다, 알고 있다
9	black	검은색; 검은
10	skate	스케이트를 타다
11	drop	떨어지다, 떨어뜨리다
12	sneakers	운동화
13	classroom	교실
14	skip	깡충깡충 뛰다
15	flood	홍수
16	sign	표지판; 서명하다
17	frog	개구리
18	knit	뜨다, 뜨개질을 하다
19	crab	게
20	comb	빗

D 1 sneezing 2 blossom 3 front
4 drums 5 foreign 6 wrong

E 1 막다, 차단하다 2 dream
3 스케치; 스케치하다 4 spider
5 두드리다, 노크하다 6 friend 7 작은
8 speak 9 크레용 10 resign 11 폭탄
12 flour 13 꽃 14 frame 15 손목, 팔목
16 fruit 17 뱀 18 lamb
19 닦다, 청소하다; 깨끗한 20 playground

F 1 plant 2 frost 3 snow 4 knees
5 smooth 6 writing 7 blind 8 created

G 1 knight 2 thumb 3 club 4 from
5 drawer 6 flute 7 space 8 Smoke
9 skirt 10 design